THE CALL TO LOVE

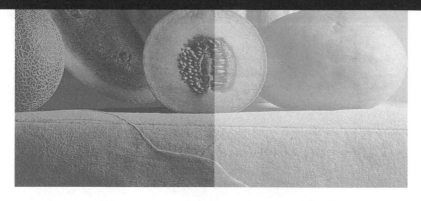

LINDA RILEY

TYNDALE HOUSE PUBLISHERS, INC. | WHEATON, ILLINOIS

Visit Tyndale's exciting Web site at www.tyndale.com

The Call to Love: Living the Great Commandments

An account of the nightmare described in chapter 7 was previously published in the winter 1997 issue of *Leadership Journal.*

The story of Frances and her dress in chapter 9 was previously published in *Leadership Journal* and in *Christian Reader,* both published by Christianity Today, Inc.

The story of the author's encounter with Yolanda in chapter 14 was previously published in the winter 1996 issue of *Leadership Journal.*

Designed by Jackie Noe
Edited by Susan Taylor and Lynn Vanderzalm

Library of Congress Cataloging-in-Publication Data

Riley, Linda
   The call to love ; living the great commandments / by Linda Riley.
      p. cm.
   ISBN 0-8423-3787-3 (sc)
   1. Love—Religious aspects—Christianity. I. Title.

BV4639 .R535 2000
241′.4—dc21   00-037785

Printed in United States of America

06 05 04 03 02 01 00
 7   6   5   4   3   2

I DEDICATE THIS BOOK TO DARWIN WILSON.
Thirty years ago a child of the light ventured into the dark to tell me
that Jesus loves me. This has made an eternity of difference to me.

Be imitators of God, therefore, as dearly loved children and live a life of love, just as Christ loved us and gave himself up for us as a fragrant offering and sacrifice to God. EPHESIANS 5:1-2

CONTENTS

ACKNOWLEDGMENTS

I wish to thank the love of my life, my husband, Jay Riley, for his help, his encouragement, and his example of love.

I wish to thank the delight and joy of my life, my children, who have taught me so much about love. Autumn, Amanda, Alexandra, Ruth, Bob, Stephen, Rachel, and Elizabeth, I am thankful for the privilege of loving you.

I wish to thank my parents, Bob and Ruth Dalton, for their constant encouragement of my writing since I was very young. I dearly love you.

Thank you to the readers of my first draft, who bravely risked our friendship to make this a better book—Thurleen Anderson, Pam Farrell, and Linda Swanson.

I am grateful for the help of all the servants of Christ at Tyndale House Publishers, especially Douglas Rumford, who believed in me and encouraged me—not for months but for years—with great patience and optimism. Thank you for the great gift of this opportunity. Many thanks to my editors, Susan Taylor and Lynn Vanderzalm, for vastly improving this book with their friendly and insightful editing skills.

Thank you to all who prayed for me and for this book during its writing and editing, my friends and colaborers all over the world, and my little flock of friends at my home church, Living Word Fellowship. If there is anything helpful within, it is because of your prayers.

Thank you to my Father, God; my Savior, Jesus Christ; and my Helper, the Holy Spirit, for giving me gifts that are so much fun to share and for writing this with me.

one

HEAVENLY LOVE

what the world needs now

Have you known any great lovers of God? They are easy to recognize because great lovers of God are also great lovers of people. They are men and women who weigh their words carefully, listen thoughtfully, behave considerately, give generously, serve diligently. When you're with them, you feel warmed, enlightened, encouraged, and affirmed. When you're in need, they find a way to help. When you're discouraged, they lift your spirits and your burden. When you're rejoicing, they celebrate with you. Even when you fail, they faithfully and lovingly stand by you.

My husband, Pastor Jay Riley, is such a man. He deserves much credit for this book. He lives an exemplary life of love, sometimes suffering for loving decisions he has made at great personal cost. He demonstrates love to his family and flock by his example and by diligent teaching and reasoning. Jay listens more than he lectures. He makes unexpected visitors to his office or home feel welcome. He knows a family's children as well as he knows their parents. He "hangs out" more than he "does visitation." He gives extravagantly, overpays guest speakers, but lives modestly himself. He makes friends with everyone he meets by showing genuine interest in their lives. Even the attendant at the gas station where Jay regularly fills up the tank counts him a good friend.

Jay often challenges my self-imposed limits of love. I

remember the time he gave our second car away to a mere acquaintance in need, the time he gathered up all our vitamin supplements to take to a sick friend, or times when he gives away our teddy bear collection, one hospital visit at a time. My willingness to love has often required stretching to match his.

After a terrible division in our church, Jay preached on various aspects of love every week for more than three years. One Sunday after church I impatiently informed him that there were a few other themes in the Bible and he might like to take a look at those. He replied, "Yes, but there are none more important. I can't build further until our cracked foundation of love is repaired." He continued to preach on love until we accepted his challenge and became a more loving church. Today, Living Word Fellowship is a church known for its loving-kindness.

To live a life of love is the worthy quest of every follower of God. But this world has so many of us struggling merely to survive that love often gets lost in the chaos. If we could pause and refocus on the great law of love that Jesus commanded his followers to obey, our lives and the lives of all we encounter would be transformed in the process. This world is never going to be like heaven, where love reigns supreme. But our individual lives can shine the light of love into dark places.

It requires a great deal of either faith or pomposity for a flawed, often less than loving human being to presume to write a book on living a life of love. My failures to love, both great and small, could fill volumes. I am not qualified to write about love because I resemble Mother Teresa or Shirley Temple or any other of the brighter lights in our universe. I am just an average woman, a flawed Christian, a fellow struggler on the path, who desperately wants to love more genuinely, more deeply, more effectively.

PERSEVERING TOWARD A LIFE OF LOVE

I want to love, and I try to love, but I have been successful only in persevering toward the ideal of love, engaging in the worthy struggle to love. I have set my heart on the wonderful words of Jesus that call us to our everyday pursuit of love. I often stumble and am often deterred. Most days I'm not skipping down love's path but climbing out of a ditch. So I dust myself off and keep walking toward the goal of greater love for God and for his most-loved creation, humanity.

Jesus is our model and teacher of the royal law of love. An expert in religious law asked him:

> "Teacher, which is the most important commandment in the law of Moses?"
>
> Jesus replied, "'You must love the Lord your God with all your heart, all your soul, and all your mind.' This is the first and greatest commandment. A second is equally important: 'Love your neighbor as yourself.' All the other commandments and all the demands of the prophets are based on these two commandments." (Matthew 22:36-40, NLT)

The Message translates Jesus' response in this way:

> Jesus said, "'Love the Lord your God with all your passion and prayer and intelligence.' This is the most important, the first on any list. But there is a second to set alongside it: 'Love others as well as you love yourself.' These two commands are pegs; everything in God's Law and the Prophets hangs from them."

Seemingly simple instructions from heaven, aren't they? But as every follower of Jesus knows, the complexities of following these commandments are endless. Still, these golden laws are the supreme desire of God for all of us: that every man, woman, and child would discover God's love, would love God in return, and then would live in a way that consistently demonstrates God's love to others.

One of the marks of Christian maturity is not that Christians know more or accomplish more. It is that they love more. As we mature, we experience an ever-increasing capacity to love. We learn how to access and express God's love in our marriages, our child rearing, our work, and our friendships. Love can triumph in every arena of life. As we increase in love, our own lives will be immeasurably enriched, and the lives of those within our sphere of influence will be enriched as well.

One of the marks of Christian maturity is not that Christians know more or accomplish more. It is that they love more.

God is love. The implications of this statement are both simple and profound. God is the source of all true, authentic, unselfish, purely motivated love, and that love is readily available to everyone who believes. If God is love, then whenever love is our motivation, we are truly men and women after God's own heart. If God is love, then whenever we love selflessly, we are acting on God's behalf. If God is love, then whenever we love, we know that we are accomplishing God's will.

Love is the greatest virtue, but it works together with faith, hope, wisdom, patience, and other virtues. Love and wisdom strategize. Love and faith fight the good fight. Love and hope cheer us on. Love and patience never give up. Love and kindness bring comfort. Love and goodness produce good works. Love and generosity meet needs. Love brings all other virtues into full fruitfulness. Dwight L. Moody said concerning the fruit of the Spirit:

Joy is love exalted.
Peace is love in repose.
Long-suffering is love enduring.
Gentleness is love in society.
Goodness is love in action.
Faith is love on the battlefield.
Meekness is love in school.
And temperance is love in training.

JOHN POLLOCK, *Moody: A Biographical Portrait*

Living a life of authentic love requires courage, perseverance, humility, thoughtfulness, and sacrifice. It is a lifelong struggle, marked by the discouragement of frequent failure and
sometimes disappointment when we send love out and it does not
return. But what rewards a life of love brings! There is a wonderful law of increase at work: God has promised that we will reap
what we sow. Those who sow loving thoughts, words, and deeds will
reap a great harvest of love, both here and in the hereafter. Those
who sow love know God's smile. They help to carry unbearable
burdens. They mend broken relationships. They wrap warmth
around cold hearts.

PAUL'S LOVE POEM

Paul the apostle, a man once ruled by hatred and bigotry, was also
a man pursued by the love of God. After his dramatic, transforming encounter with Jesus on the road to Damascus, he became a
great lover of God and a great lover of souls. The love poem he
recorded in one of his letters to the Corinthians is the perfect
treatise about what God's love looks like when brothers and
sisters share it.

I begin with 1 Corinthians 12:31 because many fail to
notice the introduction to Paul's treatise on love—the fact that love
is the shining path to true excellence—and then continue with
chapter 13:

> But eagerly desire the greater gifts. And now I will show
> you the most excellent way.
>
> If I speak in the tongues of men and of angels, but have
> not love, I am only a resounding gong or a clanging
> cymbal. If I have the gift of prophecy and can fathom all
> mysteries and all knowledge, and if I have a faith that can
> move mountains, but have not love, I am nothing. If I
> give all I possess to the poor and surrender my body to the
> flames, but have not love, I gain nothing.
>
> Love is patient, love is kind. It does not envy, it does
> not boast, it is not proud. It is not rude, it is not self-
> seeking, it is not easily angered, it keeps no record of

wrongs. Love does not delight in evil but rejoices with the truth. It always protects, always trusts, always hopes, always perseveres.

Love never fails. But where there are prophecies, they will cease; where there are tongues, they will be stilled; where there is knowledge, it will pass away. For we know in part and we prophesy in part, but when perfection comes, the imperfect disappears. When I was a child, I talked like a child, I thought like a child, I reasoned like a child. When I became a man, I put childish ways behind me. Now we see but a poor reflection as in a mirror; then we shall see face to face. Now I know in part; then I shall know fully, even as I am fully known.

And now these three remain: faith, hope and love. But the greatest of these is love. (1 Corinthians 12:31–13:1-13)

As we meditate on each phrase of this love poem, we begin to see that love is not something mushy, fussy, and frilly, not merely a lovely accoutrement to the basic values of living. Rather, love is the substance of authentic, meaningful living. There is nothing passive or soft, dreamy or delicate about God's brand of love. These verses reveal a bold and courageous love, an optimistic and faith-filled love. This love is mature, strong, confident, hard-working. Although it is more concerned with motive than with action, it continues to act until it prevails. It is a victorious love. It relentlessly pursues us until we are caught up in it and conquered by it. Then the God who is love empowers us to love as he commands. When we love with the power of God, lives change— especially our own. I invite you to join me on a journey toward greater heights and depths of love.

> The Spirit will teach us to love the Word, to meditate on it and to keep it. He will reveal the love of Christ to us, that we may love him fervently and with a pure heart. Then we shall begin to see that a life in the love of Christ in the midst of our daily life and distractions is a glorious possibility and a blessed reality.
> ANDREW MURRAY, *Every Day with Andrew Murray*

Follow the way of love.
1 Corinthians 14:1

Dear Lord, I have much to learn about following your call to love.
Let me know you intimately, for you are love. Help me to
welcome your love, embrace it, and then reflect it in the world
around me. In the name of Jesus, the great lover of our souls,
amen.

two

LOOKING FOR LOVE

seeking and finding the love that is calling you

I was just seventeen when God's pursuing love found me. I had been looking for love for some time. I had even encountered it a few times, but being spiritually blind, I had failed to recognize it. Seeking and embracing cheap imitations of love had left me feeling all used up, void of any feeling but despair. In the summer of 1970 I was still wandering Golden Gate Park in San Francisco wearing flowers in my hair and looking for love among the members of the "love generation."

Taking care of myself was hard enough, but recently my younger sister had run away from home and joined me. I was having a difficult time keeping her away from bad drugs and bad characters. After almost a year on this disappointing quest for love I remembered the two people who first loved me—my parents. I wrote them a letter from a friend's run-down apartment in the Haight-Ashbury district: "Dear Mom and Dad, As you know by now, Mary has been with me for the past few months, since she ran away. I can't take care of her anymore. She said she will come home, and I want to come home with her."

The fact that all five of their teenagers hit their hormones in the late sixties was an accident of timing for our unfortunate parents. All five of us were on drugs; all five of us embraced the current rock-and-roll rhetoric; and all five of us rejected anyone over a certain age or in authority. I had not needed to run away

9

from home. Several months before my younger sister's departure my own rebellious and troublesome behavior had caused my parents to invite me to leave. In the climate of the late sixties many parents of teenagers held little hope of a happy home life.

With my fifteen-year-old sister, Mary, tagging along on my freewheeling adventures, I began to see just how "free" and full of "love and peace" my hippie lifestyle really was. I was tired of using free love just to have a place to sleep at night. I was tired of lost young people pretending to be wise. I was tired of colorful posters about noble values that didn't translate into real life. I was tired of looking for love among the remnants of the love children. I felt achingly old and empty and couldn't generate love for anyone. My relationships reeked of neediness and desperation and came to hasty conclusions. I was desperate enough to go home and see if there was any love back in the real world.

Mary and I hitchhiked five hundred miles down Pacific Coast Highway to Torrance, California. The first week we were home my parents went away on a business trip, and we threw an "acid party," spiking Kool-Aid with LSD and stealing the ingredients for a "psychedelic" cake of five different colors and flavors. Our party only pointed out that we didn't quite fit in with our former high school crowd anymore.

Conflict marred our first few days at home. Accustomed to being at concerts at the Fillmore until two in the morning every weekend, we weren't used to ten-o'clock curfews. Our parents were angry at us for rebelling, and we were angry at them for not coming to rescue us from ourselves. I set my heart on mere survival and gave up on love.

"DID YOU KNOW THAT JESUS LOVES YOU?"

Two weeks after coming home, Mary and I hitchhiked to the beach on a Sunday afternoon. As we walked along the shore, a young man with a Bible approached us.

"Did you know that Jesus loves you?" he asked earnestly.

I answered honestly. "No, I don't know much about Jesus." Part of me wanted to leave, considering it extremely uncool to be seen with a member of "the establishment" with a Bible in his hand. But his shining face, the intensity in his clear blue eyes, and the plea in his voice made me unable to flee. I didn't know if Jesus loved me, but I thought I recognized real love and concern in this young man's eyes.

I didn't know if Jesus loved me, but I thought I recognized real love and concern in this young man's eyes.

He told us the story that proved Jesus' love, about his payment for my sins on the cross, his acceptance of me as I am, and his desire to show his love to me. I heard the whole story of salvation that day, but only parts of it touched me. I didn't care at all about escaping hell or preparing for heaven. I needed help with this life on earth, and this young man was offering me hope that I might finally find sincere, selfless, true love.

I declined to pray with our new friend or to go to church that evening, wanting time to think about his invitation to a changed life. But I did give him my phone number and agreed to attend church with him a few days later.

I felt hopeful and fearful at the same time. Mary kept questioning: What if it isn't real? What if it's just another religion, a bunch of rules? Who needs that? I tearfully demanded she stop asking so many questions. I *wanted* this story of God's love to be true, a story with a happy ending. We hitchhiked home right away so that I could find a Bible and read the truth for myself. The flirtatious boys who offered us a ride held no attraction for us, and for the first time in years we refused an offer to share drugs. Finally home, I ran into the house and asked my startled mother for a Bible. She found one, a dusty King James Version. Not knowing any better, I began at the beginning, in the book of Genesis, and I persevered through each *thee* and *thou*. By Wednesday I had read all of Genesis and Exodus, and in those first two books of the Old Testament I clearly saw God's power, his sacrificial love toward humanity, and his right to rule my life.

GOD KEEPS CALLING UNTIL WE ANSWER

Wednesday night came, and our new friend took us to Bethel Tabernacle in Redondo Beach, a Jesus movement church filled to overflowing with young people. After each testimony or song inviting us to meet Jesus, we eagerly asked our new friend, "Can we pray and meet Jesus now?" Finally the altars were opened for prayer, and we both rushed forward without so much as a glance to see if the other was coming. The pastor took my hand and said a simple prayer that I repeated after him: "Jesus, please forgive me for all the wrong things I've done. I believe that you are the Son of God and that you died on the cross to pay my debt of sin. Come live in my heart and help me to know you." Then several young people continued to pray with me. A refreshing wave of cleansing and relief washed over me. The warmth of God's love melted the icy exterior of my heart, freeing me to love and be loved. From that day forward I began to experience and grow in love. I began to understand 1 John 4:19: "We love because he first loved us." It is the love of Christ that inspires and empowers a response of love within us. I began to tell everyone I knew about the love of God and my new friend Jesus. And I was surprised that others could hear of such a wonderful heavenly Father and not embrace him!

The church where I met God had an altar where the young people could surrender items from their old ways of life. There I placed my remaining supply of birth-control pills, my hallucinogenic drugs, my rock-and-roll albums, even my hippie beads. It took me a few weeks to shake off some old boyfriends and to clean up the profane way I expressed myself. But those outward changes took no effort at all compared with the inward changes that were still necessary. The Holy Spirit began to convict me of less-obvious sins: manipulation, anger, distrust, unforgiveness, supreme selfishness, and stubborn pride. I began to see that my greatest sin was a lack of love.

Reading God's Word (having been pointed to the New Testament by now) gave me a mirror that more accurately reflected who I was in relation to God and others. I cringed at my self-centeredness, my lack of awareness of others' feelings or needs. I could hardly see beyond myself. I felt ashamed at how low my supplies of love really were. I began to notice that I always thought of myself first. The epitome of teenage self-centeredness, I had to be in control all of the time. I insisted on sitting in the front seat of the car. If we went to an amusement park, I chose all the rides. I didn't do the dishes or anything else for the rest of my family unless someone asked me to. In short, I did what was easiest for me.

As I began to see my own laziness and thoughtlessness, I also began to pray for change from within: "God, make me aware of other people's feelings and needs. Teach me how to help and encourage others. Give me more love to share with the people you put into my life." Whenever I told Jesus that I loved him, it sounded presumptuous to me, as if I knew how to love or was capable of loving him enough. I learned to pray, "Jesus, I love you with all I have, but it is not enough. Help me to love you more." Over time I began to see that we become what we pray. *Prayers for love create people who love.*

A NEW FAMILY AND A NEW LIFE

For me, the greatest thing about meeting Jesus is not my eternal home in heaven or his transforming power or all the answers to prayer I have witnessed. For almost thirty years I have seen Jesus rescue me from accidents, deliver me from troubles, provide abundantly more than I need to live, and even heal me of cancer. I'm thankful for these many gifts of his love. But I treasure most the very first gift God gave me on the day I met him—the gift of forgiveness and belonging in the family of God. God made me an adopted daughter of the most benevolent King. He makes me feel and experience his love for me so deeply that I actually feel as if I'm his favorite child even though I know that his love is perfect and does not play favorites. I can trust him with every aspect of my life because I know he always works lovingly on my behalf. And I'm profoundly thankful for the ability he gives me to love others and to enjoy the love that others show to me.

SECURE IN GOD'S LOVE

How does one learn to enjoy the Father's love? It took me a long time to truly be able to rest in his love. At first I loved him with the human motivation of wanting him to love me back. I tried to please him and earn his love through good deeds and religious rituals. I did good works for others from wrong motivations—wanting those people to value me and to reciprocate.

The first time I began to understand "what God really wants," I had believed in Jesus and had been trying to follow him for about a year. I had been taught to read the Bible and pray in the mornings, but this was a particularly busy time, filled with work and studying for night-class finals. As a week went by without my usual morning meetings with God, I felt hounded by the Holy Spirit. I knew God wanted to talk, but it was hardly convenient. I was busy about the world's business and considered this incessant pursuing by the Holy Spirit to be bothersome. One night, finally home for the evening at about ten o'clock, I finally surrendered and knelt by my bed, steeling myself for a shameful time of repentance, and began my prayers with an exasperated "All right, God, here I am."

Suddenly a feeling of indescribable warmth and well-being enveloped me. I felt as if I were wrapped in pure love and light. Jesus seemed to whisper, *Linda, I've been pursuing you because I just wanted to spend time with you.* Instead of exposing my prayerless, careless attitude, he covered me with a blanket of love that I can still feel in my memories.

When we run from God, he runs after us. God wants from us what every father wants, what every brother or sister wants, what every friend wants, what every spouse wants: He wants us to welcome his love and love him in return. Invite his love into your life. It's the first step in a great adventure of faith, hope, and love.

God, Thou art love. I build my faith on that.
ROBERT BROWNING, *Paracelsus*

This is how God showed his love among us: He sent his one and only Son into the world that we might live through him. This is love: not that we loved God, but that he loved us and sent his Son as an atoning sacrifice for our sins.
1 JOHN 4:9-10

Dear Lord, make me secure in your love. Help me to move beyond ceremony, beyond good works, beyond ritual, and embrace a faith that demonstrates love for you and for humanity. Cause me to enjoy sweet and simple fellowship with you today and every day. In the name of Jesus, amen.

three

THE GREAT COMMANDMENTS TO LOVE

making the ideal real in our everyday lives

There is no aspect of life that could not be improved by applying more love. Think how much more the world would resemble heaven if God's love became the chief ingredient in our friendships, our marriages, our work, the way we rear our children, the way we spend our leisure time, our involvement in politics, sports—in every aspect of our lives. Only the intervention of the Father's love can overcome the problems that cause so much pain, despair, and trouble: loneliness, abandonment, cruelty, rebellion, rejection, lawlessness, divorce, adultery, abuse, crime, racism, even petty meanness. The light of God's love vanquishes every evil and dark thing.

The two great commandments, to love the Lord and to love our neighbors as ourselves, usher in this overcoming love. These commandments are the key to infusing the supernatural power of God's love into our everyday lives.

WHAT THE WORLD NEEDS NOW

Jesus said, "I am giving you a new commandment: Love each other. Just as I have loved you, you should love each other. Your love for one another will prove to the world that you are my disciples" (John 13:34-35, NLT).

The church, the body of Christ made up of every follower of Christ, needs to be transformed into the lighthouse of love God meant it to be. Peruse the shelves of any Christian bookstore, and you will see how we've placed our emphasis on other admirable pursuits and qualities of godly living and Christian practice: church administration, political activism, family values, the gifts of the Spirit, the fruit of the Spirit, the discipline of prayer, the healing of pain, spiritual warfare, the art of leadership, faith that overcomes, abundant joy, the search for peace, and many other worthy topics. If love is the most important and overarching quality of Christian life, shouldn't we see more books and conferences designed to inspire the church to greater heights of love?

It is encouraging to note that love is becoming a more frequent theme in Christian literature and music. It begins where it should, with God's great love for us and our comfort in and enjoyment of his love. This renewed emphasis on love is now maturing into more thoughtfulness concerning our loving response to God and our call to love others all over the world. I believe and hope that this emphasis on love, accompanied by truth, will bring a great harvest of souls into the kingdom. As we work toward that goal of love, we need to keep some principles in mind.

POWERFUL PRINCIPLES FOR EVERYDAY CHOICES

The Ten Commandments are the cornerstone of Judeo-Christian law and practice. Jesus condensed all the law and the teachings of the prophets into two commandments, the most important and essential of all his teachings. We do well to memorize the Ten Commandments, but we can obey the ten by keeping the two great commandments in mind:

> One of the teachers of the law . . . asked [Jesus], "Of all the commandments, which is the most important?"
> "The most important one," answered Jesus, "is this: 'Hear, O Israel, the Lord our God, the Lord is one. Love the Lord your God with all your heart and with all your soul and with all your mind and with all your strength.' The second is this: 'Love your neighbor as yourself.' There is no commandment greater than these."
> (Mark 12:28-31)

These commandments are the essence of Christian living, the fundamentals of a life of faith, the foundation of godliness. They are designed to be the guiding laws of government, the most important instructions for daily living, the paramount principles for church growth and administration, the greatest guidelines for parenting, the key factors in everything we do. Every decision we make is to be weighed on the balance of love.

To practice love daily, moment by moment, may seem overwhelming. But God doesn't give his commandments to frustrate us in our failures. We have a Partner who knows just how to love, and he will show us the way. God's grace will equip us for the task of love. We can love as Jesus loved as long as we keep our eyes on the Father, as Jesus did, and our hearts set on doing his will. God grants the power to love to all who ask. If we are faithful to choose the way of love, we will reap what we sow in our families, our businesses, our ministries, and most important, in the eternal fate of our souls and the souls of those we influence.

PRINCIPLE I: LOVE GOD WITH ALL YOU ARE

God asks that we love him with the entirety of our heart, soul, mind, and strength. In the beginning of our love relationship with God, we give him a heart that is deceitfully wicked, a soul that is lost, a mind corrupted by sin, and what little strength is left after pursuing our own pleasures. That's all we have to offer.

Then God does something miraculous. He takes our paltry offerings and transforms them into something worthy of his name. He takes our hard hearts and makes them soft and pure. Through adoption into his family he anchors our lost souls. He gives us the mind of Christ. He renews our strength like the eagle's. He does not just cooperate with our old selves to make us more loving. No, the old self, what the Bible calls the flesh, must die daily. We must be born again and then continually be renewed in the Spirit to live a life of love. If we are alive in God, he gives us the love that we then return to him. Love permeates the life of the Christian.

The ways we express love will be individual and unique for each of us. God delights in distributing gifts and talents to his people. We honor and glorify him by using those talents to love and bless him and others. If you can dance, dance for the Lord. If you have artistic talent, decorate God's world. If you can cook and bake, set out a banquet for those God loves. Show your love for God in your own unique ways, using the gifts and talents God has granted you.

Those who love God don't just talk about it; their way of life shows that they love God. A life of love for God is a life of obedience to his Word. Jesus said, "If you love me, you will obey what I command" (John 14:15). John further instructs,

> "We know that we have come to know him if we obey his commands. The man who says, 'I know him,' but does not do what he commands is a liar, and the truth is not in him. But if anyone obeys his word, God's love is truly made complete in him. This is how we know we are in him: Whoever claims to live in him must walk as Jesus did." (1 John 2:3-6)

Obedience simply out of a sense of obligation to God resembles servitude more than love. True Christlike obedience must be accompanied by emotion. At times our feelings will encompass passion, joy, thankfulness, admiration, awe, affection, humility, true worship. At other times, we may feel little passion and act in love only out of dedication and commitment to God. This, too, is love. But God is our Father, and like any father, he desires more than rote adherence to rules. How many of us would be pleased with a child who obeyed our every direction but never smiled up at us or crawled into our laps or shared his latest discovery or talked to us about the things that matter to him? God desires interaction, affection, admiration, respect, relationship—God desires that we love him with all we are, all we feel, and all we possess.

PRINCIPLE 2: OUR LOVE FOR OTHERS COMES FROM OUR LOVE FOR GOD

Our love for others demonstrates our love for our heavenly Father: "We know what real love is because Christ gave up his life for us. And so we also ought to give up our lives for our Christian brothers and sisters. But if anyone has enough money to live well, and sees a brother or sister in need and refuses to help—how can God's love be in that person?" (1 John 3:16-17, NLT).

Sacrificial love for others is what the second commandment is all about. If we say we love God but we don't love others, our love for God is suspect. When we love our neighbors as ourselves, we are truly following in Jesus' footsteps. We love ourselves by nurturing our relationship with God, caring for our bodies, improving our minds, safeguarding our souls. We love others in the same way, by helping to care for their physical, emotional, and spiritual needs, by forgiving, bearing with, serving, giving, encouraging, praying, and sometimes rebuking. Love meets the other's greatest need. A life of love is beautifully unique for each of us, but there are some general principles that apply to everyone.

PRINCIPLE 3: WE CAN APPLY THE TWO GREAT COMMANDMENTS TO EVEN THE SMALLEST DECISIONS

No decision is so small that we cannot apply the test of love to the process. At first, making a conscious effort to examine our motives in the light of love can seem tedious. But the more we practice doing that, the more likely we are to make decisions that are in line with God's love.

Even a small failure of love can rob others of peace and happiness. One summer day my nephew, Bob, and my son Stephen were on their way out the door to go swimming at the community pool. Bob asked to take two towels instead of the one I offered. Thinking of the extra laundry, I replied that one would have to do. He pleaded with me, which immediately sent me into a "stand firm, Mom" mode. A frustrated, unhappy little boy walked to the pool with one towel. As soon as they left, my "Mom's in charge" defenses went down, and I regretted my decision. A moment of thoughtfulness would have helped Bob feel that his needs had been met. It would have meant more laundry, but it would also have made Bob feel more loved.

Failures of love are not wasted if they remind us to

take a moment for loving evaluation before we respond to others. If we respond automatically, the response is more likely to be self-serving. If we react with thoughtfulness, we are more likely to consider others' needs and feelings in the light of love. God is patient, and he will train us to become more loving disciples.

One early morning I caught myself in another failure to show love. As I was driving to the bank, a car cut into my lane, forcing me to a sudden near stop to accommodate the other driver's intrusion. I caught his eye in his rearview mirror, frowned, rolled my eyes, and shook my head in mock disbelief. After delivering this "You are a driving moron" message, I smugly continued on to my destination.

Then I felt guilty. Hadn't I just prayed and read my Bible that morning and asked to be more like Jesus? Sometimes we need to translate "What would Jesus do?" into "How would Jesus drive?" I can't imagine Jesus treating a rude driver rudely. So I repented and asked the Lord to help me respond to everyone I met that day in a pleasant and respectful way. I didn't know how exhausted I would be by the end of my day from all the opportunities for practice God granted me!

As I filled out my deposit slip at the bank, I noticed a new security guard standing nearby and engaged him in conversation. Soon I knew about his wife, his children, his first wife, his past job, how he got this job, what he likes to do on weekends, and the state of his spiritual health. I finally excused myself and did my banking, where the teller animatedly told me all about her church after asking about mine, since she saw the church address on my husband's paycheck. Then the new security guard caught me again on my way out. An hour after arriving at the bank I was off on other errands. I continued to make new friends at the grocery store, the cleaners, and the school. My hour of errands turned into a day of errands, but I was learning something important. Chuck Swindoll writes in *God's Provision in Time of Need:* "The wonderful thing about God's schoolroom . . . is that we get to grade our own papers. You see, He doesn't test us so He can learn how well we're doing. He tests us so *we* can discover how well we're doing."

Answering the call to love involves a commitment to receive training from the Lord and a willingness to start over again each time we fail.

Answering the call to love involves a commitment to receive training from the Lord and a willingness to start over again each time we fail.

Often the Lord retrains us just to give us back our confidence in who we really are in him. I once caused myself much grief by making a lazy and selfish choice that resulted in financial cost to others. In response, the Lord immediately began testing me in this area. Clerks consistently gave me too much change, forcing me to return to rectify the matter. I found over two hundred dollars on the floor in a grocery store and needed to turn it in. I then found several hundred dollars in a parking lot and had the opportunity to turn that in to the nearest store. Situations involving money and integrity continued for a few months and then suddenly ceased. The Lord was strengthening me by testing an area in my life where I had shown weakness. The Lord is merciful not only to forgive but also to rebuild our confidence about choosing what is loving and right.

Even though we may be inclined to be gracious and help everyone, we need to take time to evaluate requests for our time and resources. Love walks hand in hand with wisdom, and we must pray for both. Sometimes asking ourselves questions can help us to evaluate a request for our help.

Do I Need More Time to Think about This Request?

Do you tend to automatically say yes when someone makes a request of you? People love to hear that response. In fact, those who say yes quickly and often usually find themselves very popular, especially with volunteer groups! It may help to remember that God does not say yes to every request we make. Sometimes he says no or asks us to wait.

When fulfilling a request would require significant time,

attention, or resources, it can be helpful to say something like, "Thank you for asking. Let me take a look at my calendar," or "Let me think about it [or discuss it with my spouse, or whatever], and I'll get back to you on that." Then I can take time to make a prayerful decision about whether this request is something I should commit to.

Would My Help Benefit That Person Long Term?

A coworker may want help with an upcoming report, but if that person makes the same request every time a report is due, I may do her more good by going over the procedure briefly and then excusing myself when she asks the next time so that she can learn and gain confidence from the experience of doing the report herself.

My child may want to run out to the ice-cream truck on a summer afternoon, but if I evaluate his request in light of the fact that I want him to have a good appetite for dinner, I may turn down his request, preferably with an explanation about why.

Sometimes we say no to ourselves because we evaluate the long-term benefit of what we want. We may say no to a second cookie because we want to enjoy the long-term benefits that come from a healthful diet. We may forego buying something we *want* because it would be a better use of the money to provide what someone else *needs*. We may say no to things that seem wonderful for the moment because we evaluate those things from a long-term perspective.

God's love considers the present in light of the future.

PRINCIPLE 4: WE CAN OBEY THE GREATEST COMMANDMENTS IN ANY CIRCUMSTANCES

In *A Book of Saints*, Anne Gordon tells the story of love's victory in even the most hellish of environments. Father Maximilian Kolbe was a prisoner at Auschwitz in 1941 when another prisoner escaped. The Nazis retaliated by sentencing ten prisoners to die of starvation. Father Kolbe offered to take the place of one of the condemned men. The Nazis accepted the offer and starved Kolbe for two weeks before finally executing him by lethal injection on August 14, 1941.

Thirty years later a survivor of Auschwitz described the effect of Kolbe's action:

> It was an enormous shock to the whole camp. We became aware that someone among us in this spiritual dark night of the soul was raising the standard of love on high. Someone unknown, like everyone else, tortured and bereft of name and social standing, went to a horrible death for the sake of someone not even related to him. Therefore it is not true, we cried, that humanity is cast down and trampled in the mud, overcome by oppressors, and overwhelmed by hopelessness. Thousands of prisoners were convinced the true world continued to exist and that our torturers would not be able to destroy it.
>
> To say that Father Kolbe died for us or for that person's family is too great a simplification. His death was the salvation of thousands. . . . We were stunned by his act, which became for us a mighty explosion of light in the dark camp.

Living in America and enjoying religious freedom, we don't often consider all the varied circumstances under which people faithfully serve the Lord. We don't have to have abundant resources, perfect health, or even religious freedom to love others fully. Many great lovers of the Lord live in poverty, ill health, or under persecution. While we talk about struggling to love our mother-in-law, others struggle to love the prison guards who torture and deprive them and have separated them from their families. Modern-day martyrs are a fact of Christian life, and we ought never to forget our brothers and sisters imprisoned, persecuted, and murdered for their faith in Jesus. Others are giving their very lives while we can barely surrender a Sunday morning to the Lord.

Sometimes all someone is able to do for others is pray, but this is one of the greatest ministries to which we can devote ourselves. I know of a bedridden elderly woman who prays daily in response to what she hears on the news. She prays for every grieving family. She prays for lost children until they are found. She prays for political leaders. This is her act of service to Christ and his loved ones. She does not allow her illness to dictate her level of commitment. She has found something she can do under any circumstances—she can love and pray.

Corrie ten Boom served the Lord faithfully in a Nazi concentration camp. Joni Eareckson Tada has invested every talent she's been given, singing, writing, speaking, painting, and more, while spending most of her life in a wheelchair. Never say that you aren't strong enough, that you don't have something to share. God has given us so much. He grants everyone some "talents" of love (Matthew 25). I've seen homeless people sharing their food in the park. Someone gave them a little, and they shared it. We need to relentlessly search for opportunities to share love. Let's ask God to show us how to love within our circumstances. We don't have to wait until we have more or know more or are in "a better position." Let's get in the kneeling position and ask for ideas on how to love others with the resources God gives us, in the circumstances where he places us.

We don't have to wait until we have more or know more or are in "a better position." Let's get in the kneeling position and ask for ideas on how to love others with the resources God gives us, in the circumstances where he places us.

PRINCIPLE 5: THE GREAT COMMANDMENTS MAKE "KINGDOM SENSE," NOT COMMON SENSE

If you make the greatest commandments the governing law of your life, your choices and decisions may sometimes defy common sense. They may cause your relatives or business associates to wonder about your sanity. Sometimes a loving decision will cost you money or the respect of someone you admire. Sometimes even the recipient of your loving decision will say it doesn't make sense.

A ministry I directed for many years was involved in publishing. We published books, pamphlets, newsletters, a catalog, and the usual letterhead, mailing labels, brochures, and business cards. Early on I found a good printer. Kenny Lerner was a wonderful Christian brother, and his bids were on target, his advice beneficial, and he got all our jobs out on time for more than a decade.

For one job I used a graphic artist to help design a new resource catalog. It was more complicated and colorful than our usual pieces, so she suggested I get a bid from a large printing house that had more sophisticated equipment. I did and then submitted the job to Kenny for his price quote. Kenny came in at seventeen hundred dollars over the competitor's bid to print ten thousand catalogs. The printing business had changed, and Kenny wasn't able to compete with those who had all the latest equipment. He sadly informed me that he couldn't do the job for any less and graciously urged me to use the new printing house.

I acquiesced, but I didn't feel right about it. That night I discussed it with Jay, and we decided that love and loyalty are more important than money. Kenny needed the work, and he should have it. But this ministry was a nonprofit organization, and I needed to be a good steward with the sacrificial gifts others had made to the ministry. How could I spend more than was absolutely necessary to get the job done? Jay and I decided to make a donation so that it would be our sacrifice, not the donors'. It wasn't easy, but we felt the Lord would honor it.

The next day I called Kenny. "Kenny, we'd like to stick with you on the catalog job. I'll get the disk to you this afternoon."

"What?! Why?"

"I'm going with you because we love you and you love us and we've been working together for a long time."

"You're kidding."

"No, I'm not. The job is yours."

"Well, thank you. I need the work."

"You always do a great job," I answered. "See you this afternoon."

I did not know it then, but had we abandoned Kenny at

that time, it would have felt to him as if we were pounding one more nail into his coffin. He told me later that he had lost most of his accounts to the larger printing houses. Soon after this, when we learned that his business was about to close, Jay and I went to pray with him and discovered how encouraged he had felt to have one account choose to remain when he was losing so many others. What is love and encouragement worth? It's easily worth more than seventeen hundred dollars.

In a business sense, and in a personal financial sense, our decision seemed foolish. In God's economy it was a wise invest- ment. Love is willing to appear foolish—and even to suffer loss— for the sake of another.

We must learn to listen carefully to the voice of love. I do not necessarily follow through on every good intention and sweet idea. I follow through only when I know I'm following God's gentle direction. The more we listen, obey, and act in faith, the more God will trust us with risky assignments. Love often leads to a path that is foreign and unfamiliar in the eyes of the world. But the great law of love is supreme over all, even over common sense and worldly wisdom.

PRINCIPLE 6: LOVE IS A HUMBLE WALK THROUGH EVERYDAY CHOICES

Following Jesus on the path of love is an adventure requiring a daily commitment. We fall down often. But the next morning we can rise up with fresh determination and try again. We can try to give every person we meet a glimpse of God's love and power, a reason to believe in love.

Everyday love is courteous, generous, kind, and patient. It is considerate, treating others with dignity and respect. A day of love might look like this: You let the driver into your lane even if she is crowding you. You invite the person with only three items to move in front of you in the grocery store line. When a child is selling something, you buy something. When your coworker is grumpy occasionally, you let her be grumpy and pretend you don't notice. When you get a traffic ticket, you sincerely apologize for not doing your job and thank the officer for doing hers. You explain the rules patiently every time your four-year-old breaks them. You say no to the curfew extension for your teenager and then explain why. You give your boss a full day's work. You don't flirt with anyone but your spouse. You stop and chat with your neighbor on the way to your car. You bake cookies with your twelve-year-old, hoping she'll reveal what is behind her moodiness. You relinquish the coveted remote control. That's everyday love.

Mother Teresa said, "We can do no great things, only small things with great love." Real love lived out in our real world is rarely spectacular. Sometimes all it means is that you muster all your strength to calm yourself and not yell at your sister when she richly deserves it. Sometimes it means going for a walk with your friend even though you don't really feel like it. Sometimes it means listening patiently and waiting to say something wise when you'd rather reply, "Grow up, already!" Authentic love is the result of a series of choices to live selflessly.

SOMETIMES LOVE REQUIRES EXTRAORDINARY EFFORT

Sometimes God will give us opportunities to show extraordinary love, spectacular love, love well beyond reason, love that is costly and demanding. This kind of love may buy a bigger house than your family needs because you want to set up a guest room for traveling friends and those who need a cost-free respite. This kind of love ministers through meals, gifts, reading aloud, and other kindnesses to someone who is terminally ill. This costly love reaches out with forgiveness and God's grace to a criminal behind bars who victimized your family. This love adopts hard-to-place physically or mentally challenged youngsters. Extraordinary love takes many forms, but it is easily recognizable. When we hear of it, our mouths drop open, we're left speechless, and we wonder, *Could I ever do anything like that?* You never know what you are capable of doing until you are asked to do it. You can do anything Jesus asks you to, for every heavenly request is accompanied by sufficient grace and the power source of God's love.

Extraordinary love gives extravagantly, or requires vast

amounts of time and energy, or demands that your own goals wait while you help others reach theirs. These acts of love change the course of others' lives. When God presents remarkable opportunities to love, accept them as a gift to others and to yourself. We need to open God's gift of opportunity and discover memorable, exciting, challenging, rewarding experiences that can become the highlights of our lives.

This world cries, "Every man for himself!" Christians cry, "All for one and one for all!" An everyday life lived in love can make that cry a reality.

> Our responsibility as Christians is to discover the meaning of this command and seek passionately to live it out in our daily lives.
> MARTIN LUTHER KING JR., COMMENTING ON THE COMMAND
> TO LOVE ONE ANOTHER, IN *Strength to Love*

As the Father has loved me, so have I loved you. Now remain in my love. If you obey my commands, you will remain in my love, just as I have obeyed my Father's commands and remain in his love. I have told you this so that my joy may be in you and that your joy may be complete. My command is this: Love each other as I have loved you. Greater love has no one than this, that he lay down his life for his friends.
JOHN 15:9-13

Dear Lord, help me to revere the great commandments in my heart and my mind. Let your love triumph in each small act, in every decision. Fill my days with your love, and give me courage for the times you ask of me an even greater measure of love. Make me a willing sacrifice. In the name of Jesus, who laid down his own life, amen.

four

LOVE IS A WORTHY STRUGGLE

winning the daily battle between love and selfishness

I lie down on a comfortable couch and struggle uncomfortably between love and selfishness, not knowing which will triumph; they're both so strong. Cozy and warm in my sister's home in San Francisco, I hold no desire to venture into the rain and my own pain to find my brother. He's so difficult to find.

We lost my brother Danny a long time ago. The fading family photographs in my sister's living room hold no clues. I look at him, a three-year-old cherub, smiling sweetly into my newborn face, delighted to be the big brother of twins. I look at my ten-year-old mischief-making brother, proudly tugging his red wagon "float" in a local Fourth of July parade. I see him as a sailor, skimming the Pacific with my dad, winning third place in the race to Catalina Island. I search the fading memories of my warm, witty, kindhearted, fun-loving brother and wonder how he could disappear so irrevocably.

He first slipped away at about twenty years old. He became confused and troubled, hallucinating, relating improbable plots and fanciful tales, angrily accusing us, then pitifully apologizing. Gradually the frightening mask of mental illness grew horrifyingly recognizable as it concealed more and more of my brother's likeness. Danny was diagnosed with schizophrenia.

While we were growing up, loving Danny was easy, joyful, carefree. Since mental illness overtook him, loving Danny turned

31

privately painful. I can't navigate in Danny's world, a realm of paranoia, nonexistent threats, voices that echo only in his mind, behavior that no sane person can explain or predict. I can only venture near the edges and try to find my lost brother inside this near stranger.

My sister Sylvia lives on San Francisco's Telegraph Hill, near Danny, and often sees him in the middle of some city street, gesturing wildly, arguing with Mr. Invisible. One day Sylvia called me. "I saw Danny today, stumbling into a downtown store. He didn't even know there was blood all over his forehead. I pulled the car over and cried." I got off the phone quickly, before she could hear me weep for our lost brother. She wept alone when she saw it. I wept alone when I heard it. We each feel a lonely grief and try not to touch each other where it hurts.

People seeing Danny wandering the streets may assume he is homeless and destitute of love. But he has a mom and dad who love him. He has three sisters and a brother who love him. He has nieces and nephews who pray for him at night. We all love him with an anguished love, a desperate love, a nearly helpless love.

My twin brother, Darrell, also lives nearby and sees to some of Danny's needs, checking up on him, delivering packages, and making hospital visits. Danny is often in the hospital. He disregards traffic signals or is mugged. Or he is admitted to the psychiatric ward for the mandatory three days because his bizarre behavior interrupted someone's normal life and the police came to remove the problem.

I breathe a sigh of relief when Danny is in the hospital. Then I know that for a while he will eat three meals a day instead of his usual diet of beer, cigarettes, and coffee. He will take showers and wear clean clothes. Someone will see to it that he takes his medication. For just a while he is safe from the perils of life in a strange, distorted world.

We are all relieved while he's in the hospital, all except for Danny. He prefers his independent life, wandering the city streets, carousing, and entertaining himself however he pleases. In this society even irrational people have the freedom to choose, and he has chosen to refuse long-term help.

To spare him from homelessness Sylvia's husband, Galen, managed to find him a hotel apartment. The manager doles out Danny's expense money three times a day to remind him to eat and to keep him from being mugged for larger sums of cash. Galen and Sylvia have diligently cared for Danny over the years, obtaining his disability checks and VA benefits, working with the hospital when he is admitted, and helping him negotiate some of the details of life.

Danny has succeeded in making a life for himself, more than an existence, a life of small satisfactions. He struggles, more valiantly than most, to love. He shares everything. The cookies I bake him are never hoarded but cheerfully shared with friends. He does what he can with what he is given. Still, I grieve for the adventurous life Danny would have lived if this illness had not come and stolen all that he could have been and done and enjoyed.

A FAMILY REUNION

One weekend I decided my children should finally meet their Uncle Danny. My children had prayed for him and comforted me when I cried for him, but they had never met him.

I prepared them for his appearance and behavior and assured them that they needn't be afraid, then arranged a reunion in a city park. All the grown-up brothers and sisters came together again: Sylvia, Danny, Darrell, Mary, and I. We introduced our children to their strange Uncle Danny, and then they played in the park while the grown-ups who grew up together enjoyed that love-beyond-reason that siblings share. My brother-in-law, Galen, offered to take a photo of the family. Strange sights are not uncommon in San Francisco, but this grouping must have looked especially incongruous. Perplexed onlookers stared as four apparently middle-class middle-agers gathered around a seemingly homeless, filthy, disheveled old man and yelled "Cheese!" Sylvia sent the picture to our parents, who placed it prominently in their living room.

MEAGER REMINDERS OF LOVE

I love Danny passionately from afar. There is hardly a day that I don't think about Danny, sometimes with pity and grief, sometimes with admiration for the way he faces everyday life with uncommon bravery. I search for practical ways to love him. I plead in prayer on Danny's behalf. I remember his birthday and send gifts at Christmas. Even the mentally ill know when it's Christmas and hope for remembrances.

I often send him meager reminders of love: postcards, photos, his favorite cookies. But to see him face-to-much-changed-face, to look into his distracted eyes—this requires a more courageous love.

This is why I am sitting in my sister's living room, tempted to skip my usual visit with Danny. Loving Danny is so costly. It exacts every ounce of bravery and grace I can gather. It summons all my strength to smile at Danny while I'm missing him so.

Selfishness and sacrifice argue within me: *It's OK if I don't go this time. I can visit him next time I'm in town.*

Selfishness and sacrifice argued within me: *It's OK if I don't go this time. I can visit him next time I'm in town. He will never know I was here and forfeited the chance to see him. His shabby hotel is depressing. It's a dangerous area to visit. It's difficult to talk with Danny. It hurts. I just can't do it. I don't want to look into his eyes, hold his hand, and search to find him. I can't go this time. I don't want to go. OK, I'm not going. There, that's settled.*

Whew! What relief! For about ten seconds. Then love speaks: *If you were the one in the shabby hotel, with only a few memories left lying dormant beneath the confusing voices, would you want Danny to come visit you? Would you want to be held? Would you want to hear, "I love you" from a familiar voice?*

FINDING DANNY

Love triumphs. I pray for courage and grab my coat. My brother-in-law, Galen, and I drive to Danny's hotel. He isn't there. We drive around the city, searching his favorite parks and corner hangouts. An hour passes. Now I'm desperate to find him. I reason, "Galen, God knows where Danny is. Let's pray." We hold hands and pray that we will find him. Galen suggests we go back to the hotel. Perhaps Danny has returned.

As Galen goes down the hallway to check his room, I pace the musty hotel lobby, mentally preparing myself to see Danny. I submerge my shock beneath a carefully rehearsed smile when I first see him, toothpick thin, prematurely aged, head shaved, legs crookedly misshapen from a recent collision with a car. He runs down the hall in an awkward fashion. At first I notice only the awkwardness. Then, I realize, he is *running*. He is running to me, his expression ecstatic, expectant.

Suddenly, the pain is forgotten. I have found Danny! There is enough left of my brother to come running to his sister. I'm so glad I chose to visit Danny. I throw my arms around his soiled, bony frame and hold him as long as he'll allow. Then I produce an offering of his favorite candy, malted-milk balls. A two-tooth grin spreads across his gaunt, sun-parched face. He looks much older than his forty-two years, but he smiles with a child's pleasure and shares the small gift with friends in the lobby.

We sit down and reminisce about pranks pulled and trips taken. The conversation continues in disconnected fragments, abrupt exclamations, and searching silences. Danny detours in and out of delusions and confusion. But when we speak of family memories, his eyes grow misty and look wistfully into mine. Touching and talking, I reach past his broken mind and find his still responsive heart. We sit awhile and have our difficult and satisfying visit. This is a worthy struggle, loving Danny.

When I return to Sylvia's home, my teenage niece looks up innocently and asks, "Did you enjoy your visit with Uncle Danny? Is he getting any better?" The last question startles me. No, he's not getting any better. But I am getting better at loving and accepting him the way he is. I put my arm around her and explain, "Honey, I don't think Uncle Danny is ever going to get any better. But I definitely enjoyed my visit with him today."

A BLESSED MEMORY

The story of my visit with Danny is a memory now—an important memory. That night I flew home warmly satisfied with having made the choice to visit Danny. I thought he needed my visit. I didn't know how much I needed the visit, the touches, the words, the memories. I didn't know until months later that the visit I struggled so to make would be our last visit. A few months after our time together Danny collapsed on a San Francisco street and died a few days later of pneumonia. My last chance to say "I love you" was the chance I almost forfeited. A choice to love afforded me that last opportunity to hold him, to value him, to give gifts and encouraging words. It was a worthy struggle, loving Danny.

Through his giving and caring, Danny made an impact in his own small world and left fond memories in the hearts of those who knew him. And perhaps after meeting Danny in these pages, more people will make room in their hearts and prayers for the mentally ill. Danny's life was meaningful simply because he lived, loved, and was loved.

We all have someone in our lives like Danny. Someone we so want to love, someone who longs for our love yet can't express that longing. We struggle to connect, to express our feelings, to develop a relationship. We feel frustrated because our loved one seems incapable of returning love. Love seems like an insurmountable task. Yet the goal of love is always attainable with God's help. Instead of trying to imagine a lifetime of loving that person, make one loving choice at a time. Send a gift, write a letter, make a visit, reply kindly to harsh words, forgive an offense, pray a prayer. Love in little steps, and soon you will reach your goal. A bestselling book is written one sentence at a time. A masterpiece is painted one brush stroke at a time. A beautiful life of love is formed from a series of small decisions, simple choices—choices of seemingly little consequence but weighed on the balance of love. Love is a struggle but always a worthy struggle.

> We cannot love one another too much. It is impossible to love too much. "This is my commandment that you love another as I have loved you." We cannot approach that, much less pass it, so we cannot love too much. Let all loving hearts then be at rest about loving. Only let love feel selfless, strong, brave, faithful.

There are always chances for strengthening another's hands in
God; let us not lose our chances.

Amy Carmichael, *Edges of His Ways*

Be devoted to one another in brotherly love. Honor one another above yourselves.
Romans 12:10

*Dear Lord, let love triumph in every great and small decision we
make. Enable us to love the poor, the needy, the sick, the
orphaned, the imprisoned, those on the highways and byways of
our lives, those you have asked us to gather for the banquet of
love you've prepared. In Jesus' name, amen.*

five

THE SOURCE OF LOVE

accessing endless supplies of love

I felt so embarrassed. I had been caught off guard by a question from a relative who lives a consistently moral life yet professes no faith. She was shocked by a mutual friend's sinful and selfish behavior and was trying to reconcile her actions with what she professed to believe.

"I don't understand. You say you live for Jesus and believe in the Bible," my relative observed. "Well, Louise [not her real name] says the same thing. You both go to church. You both pray before lunch every time we go out. But look at the way Louise treats people, even her own family. Look at all the damage she leaves in her wake. If Jesus shows Christians the way to live, where is Jesus in her life?"

I was embarrassed for my friend and for my faith, and I didn't know what to say. My relative's observations were accurate and devastating. Louise's selfish actions had hurt others terribly and had cast doubt on the genuineness of her faith. I prayed a quick prayer for wisdom, and an answer came. "Jesus is as close to Louise as she will allow him to be. And Jesus is as close to you and me as we will allow him to be. Unfortunately, Louise isn't making much room for Jesus in her life right now."

PERFECT LOVE IN IMPERFECT VESSELS

The fact that many professing Christians fail to walk in the footsteps of Jesus has often hindered unbelievers from seeing Jesus at work on the earth. But the fact that Christians fail to love in a Christlike way does not change one thing about the nature of God's love. It is still perfect, pure, and available to all.

The fact that Christians fail to love in a Christlike way does not change one thing about the nature of God's love.

I recall sitting on an airplane next to a kindhearted man who told me the story of how he had lost touch with God. He had once loved God and loved serving the poor. He ran a soup kitchen and food pantry for the homeless out of his church. After some time, budget considerations caused the church board to close his beloved ministry outreach. No more soup for the homeless so that the church could be remodeled for the comfort of the church members. He was so disappointed with church politics and priorities that instead of searching out other avenues of service, he stopped going to church altogether. Disappointment turned into anger, and anger into bitterness. Gradually he stopped giving to charities, praying, reading the Bible, or practicing any of the other disciplines of the Christian life that he had formerly enjoyed. He stopped going to the source of love, and soon his supply was depleted. Until we talked that day he had never thought about how he had allowed flawed people to close his heart toward his loving Father. He decided he could still love God and love people, no matter what others did, and he made a new commitment to trust God and to try to trust God's people once again.

So many have abandoned church life because of disappointment with church people. If we want to see churches become more loving, we must constantly refill our hearts with new supplies of God's love. Without God as our source, we are bankrupt of love. Our parents cannot give us enough love. Our spouses cannot give us all the love we want. Our children cannot meet our need for love. All of our friends and family put together could not satisfy our desire for love. Our need for love would be insatiable if it were not for God, whose love truly satisfies the hungriest heart, the thirstiest soul. To love as Jesus loved, we must start from a place where our own hearts are satisfied with God's love. Then we will love God in return and share his great love for humanity.

WHEN LOVE GROWS COLD

Jesus taught an alarming fact about the last days: "Because of the increase of wickedness, the love of most will grow cold" (Matthew 24:12). Notice that he said, "the love of most." We need to pray that this will not become our fate as believers. We need to pray that God will give us passionate love. Love that burns right through the dross of what this world offers. When the pervasiveness of sin and hypocrisy promotes an unhealthy pessimism, we may be tempted to think, *Another has fallen. Who can stay faithful to the end?* or *Look at what this person or that one is doing. Why shouldn't I do that, too?* Focusing on others' failings brings discouragement, and our love begins to cool. Focusing on Jesus keeps passionate love burning bright.

Sometimes we allow our love for God to grow cold through anger toward others, resentment toward God for life's circumstances, or disappointment over unanswered prayers or prayers whose answers were not what we desired. Perhaps we make prayer demands, not prayer requests, and then withhold our affection for God until he meets them. When we feel swamped by anger toward others, we need to remember that we have failed others or disappointed them, too. Then we need to release our resentment to God and accept his sovereignty in our lives. In spite of how it may feel to us at times, God is working lovingly on our behalf, even in the most painful of circumstances. When we remind ourselves that God loved us enough to sacrifice his Son for our sake, we can rest in the promise of his love for us and in the assurance that he knows what he is doing.

While a child is throwing a tantrum, he is not capable of crawling into his father's lap and resting in his father's love. That happens only after the tantrum is over and the child has accepted the father's will. When we don't feel God's affectionate nurturing, we need to examine our hearts. Have we stopped throwing tantrums? Have we asked our Father to instruct and guide us and have his way in our lives? As soon as we surrender to his will, we can crawl back into his lap and enjoy the comfort of his loving embrace.

Many people don't trust in the fact of God's love for them because an earthly father or father figure treated them so unlike the way their heavenly Father treats his children. Perhaps they had a painful experience with a church, a minister, or a person who claimed to represent Jesus Christ but disappointed them or even inflicted insult or injury. In these cases the concept of "father" may evoke feelings of pain and sadness rather than the image of a welcoming embrace and loving care. A painful experience may interfere with your ability to feel your heavenly Father's love for you.

If that is the case, don't let any thing, any person, any experience stand between you and your loving heavenly Father. You can go straight to the source of love, to God himself, and ask him to show you his love. You can ask him to help you understand his vast wealth of love for you and help you feel it in meaningful ways. Watch and listen for his answer. As the infinite Creator, God can be creative in the way he reveals himself to each person. You will become more and more aware of his love and care for you as God opens your heart and your eyes.

THE BIBLE: GOD'S LOVE LETTERS

One of the best ways to understand God's love is to become familiar with God's love letter to us, the Bible. There we find treasures beyond our capacity to spend them all! Here are just a few samples of what God says about his love for us:

From everlasting to everlasting the Lord's love is with those who fear him, and his righteousness with their children's children. (Psalm 103:17)

The Lord leads with unfailing love and faithfulness all those who keep his covenant and obey his decrees. (Psalm 25:10, NLT)

The Lord is righteous in everything he does; he is filled with kindness. (Psalm 145:17, NLT)

He brings me to the banquet hall, so everyone can see how much he loves me. (Song of Songs 2:4, NLT)

Long ago the Lord said to Israel: "I have loved you, my people, with an everlasting love. With unfailing love I have drawn you to myself." (Jeremiah 31:3, NLT)

Jesus knew that the time had come for him to leave this world and go to the Father. Having loved his own who were in the world, he now showed them the full extent of his love. (John 13:1)

Jesus replied, "All those who love me will do what I say. My Father will love them, and we will come to them and live with them." (John 14:23, NLT)

Whether we are high above the sky or in the deepest ocean, nothing in all creation will ever be able to separate us from the love of God that is revealed in Christ Jesus our Lord. (Romans 8:39, NLT)

Does that small sample inspire you to read more? Fill yourself up with the truth about God's love. The Gospel of John is a great place to begin reading about God's magnificent love story written to you.

GO DIRECTLY TO THE SOURCE OF LOVE

Sometimes we are so busy looking for answers to our problems in Christian books and on Christian radio and television programs that we don't think about getting on our knees and going directly to the Source for the love we need. God is love. Get closer to God and you will feel, experience, and know more love. You won't just know *about* love, you'll dwell *in* love. God promises that if you draw close to him, he will draw close to you (James 4:8). God's love will move right into your heart.

Probably the best way to get closer to God is to pray. Pray continually. You don't have to be eloquent. You don't have to ask in just the right way. You don't have to change your voice inflection to sound a tad more holy. You don't have to explain everything to God. Pray simply, telling God what is on your mind; then simply believe: "God, I feel very unlovable and unloved. I know

43

the Bible says you love me, but I want to feel it. Help me to know it beyond any doubt. Help me to enjoy your love. Help me to overflow with a sense of your love."

Or perhaps you know his love for you personally but you need more love for those who are a bit difficult to get along with. Then you might pray something like this: "God, I need more love. I don't have enough. Please give me a greater capacity for love. Give me love for so-and-so. Help me to always respond lovingly to that person." These are simple prayers, but any prayer prayed in sincerity enters God's throne room.

Spending time each morning refilling your vessel with the love of God through reading his Word and praying is the best way to keep overflowing with God's love. But sometimes people or circumstances use up our supplies in no time at all! That's when we need a quick refill. Pray again, asking for grace to keep on loving, for patience, for a soft answer, for whatever the situation requires. But take that moment to refill. If there is any prayer God is predisposed to answer, it's a prayer for more love. When we ask God for more love in a particular situation, it's just like personally asking God to take over, for God is love.

God's Word promises that we can grow in our "love-ability," the ability to express God's love in our world:

> As we know Jesus better, his divine power gives us everything we need for living a godly life. He has called us to receive his own glory and goodness! And by that same mighty power, he has given us all of his rich and wonderful promises. He has promised that you will escape the decadence all around you caused by evil desires and that you will share in his divine nature.

> So make every effort to apply the benefits of these promises to your life. Then your faith will produce a life of moral excellence. A life of moral excellence leads to knowing God better. Knowing God leads to self-control. Self-control leads to patient endurance, and patient endurance leads to godliness. Godliness leads to love for other Christians, and finally you will grow to have

44

genuine love for everyone. The more you grow like this, the more you will become productive and useful in your knowledge of our Lord Jesus Christ. (2 Peter 1:3-8, NLT)

Moral excellence, self-control, patient endurance, godliness, genuine love—these are worthy qualities. And God's Word says that we can possess these qualities in increasing measure! Isn't it good news that we can grow in love? Pray for an ever-increasing capacity to love. This is a prayer that pleases God and one he will faithfully answer.

JOHN, THE DISCIPLE WHOM JESUS LOVED

Do you remember the painting titled *The Last Supper*? In it the artist depicts the apostle John reclining on Jesus' shoulder. It seems John really knew how to get close to Jesus' heart. When Jesus first met up with James and John, the brothers were called "sons of thunder." But after spending three years with Jesus, John had a different title: "the disciple whom Jesus loved."

The disciple whom Jesus loved. I remembered hearing that phrase before, but I had only a vague idea about what it really meant. That's what I wanted to be, though, a disciple whom Jesus loved! So I began to make a study of the Gospel of John and the three letters John authored (cleverly titled 1 John, 2 John, and 3 John).

Of the four Gospels, John's seems to give the clearest, simplest, yet most compelling exposition of the life of Christ and the plan of salvation. Could this be because John so clearly understood Jesus' mission of love? And John wrote each of his letters with one purpose in mind: to expound on the true nature of love and to encourage dedicated love for God and sincere love among believers. Could this be because John so intimately knew the love of God found in Jesus?

Only John's Gospel tells about how Jesus probed Peter about his commitment to love. In chapter 21 John tells of the searching exchange between Peter and Jesus, who asked Peter three times, "Do you love me? Do you really love me?" Only John's Gospel includes the account of Jesus' words appointing John to be the caretaker of Mary, Jesus' widowed mother: "When Jesus saw his mother there, and the disciple whom he loved standing nearby, he said to his mother, 'Dear woman, here is your son,' and to the disciple, 'Here is your mother.' From that time on, this disciple took her into his home" (John 19:26-27). Jesus had brothers and other disciples who could have cared for his mother. But perhaps Jesus knew no one would love and care for his mother more than John would. Passionate love for Jesus produces compassionate love for the family of God.

As I studied John's life and his contributions to the Word of God, I noticed something that had previously escaped my attention. Matthew, Mark, and Luke, the other three writers of the

---

Passionate love for Jesus produces compassionate love for the family of God.

Gospel accounts, never referred to John as the disciple whom Jesus loved. Paul, Peter, James, and the other writers of the New Testament books never refer to John as the disciple whom Jesus loved. Only John refers to himself as the disciple whom Jesus loved! John bestowed the title on himself.

What confidence in Jesus' intimate, personal love for him! What an example to us! This is not a symptom of pride or pomposity but a matter-of-fact confidence in the status of his relationship with Jesus. We all need to think of ourselves as disciples whom Jesus loves. We all need to take our turn resting against Jesus' bosom as John did, getting as close as we can to the beating of his heart. It was John's closeness to the heart of Jesus and his quiet confidence in Jesus' love for him that enabled him to become the great encourager toward love that he is in all his writings.

John reassures us of God's accepting love in John 6:37, where Jesus says, "Those the Father has given me will come to me, and I will never reject them" (NLT). When we approach God, he will not reject us. Take a step toward home. Take a step toward *him*. Like the father of the Prodigal Son, when God sees a son or daughter returning from afar, he comes running. While we are

still tentatively turning toward home, God comes running to
gather us up in his arms! Come home to the Father's love. Rest
your head on Jesus' shoulder. Become a disciple whom Jesus loves.

> The whole claim of the redemption of Jesus is that He can
> satisfy the last aching abyss of the human soul, not only
> hereafter, but here and now.
>
> OSWALD CHAMBERS, *In the Presence of His Majesty*

*Dear friends, let us continue to love one another, for love comes from God. Anyone
who loves is born of God and knows God. But anyone who does not love does not
know God—for God is love.*
1 JOHN 4:7-8, NLT

*Dear Lord, I pray that we, "being rooted and established in love,
may have power, together with all the saints, to grasp how wide
and long and high and deep is the love of Christ, and to know
this love that surpasses knowledge—that [we] may be filled to
the measure of all the fullness of God." In the name of Jesus,
amen. (This perfect prayer is found in Ephesians 3:17-19.)*

six

JESUS LOVES THE LITTLE CHILDREN

lavishing love on little ones

I have never had a baby. I have never felt life move inside of me, never delivered a soul fresh from heaven, never experienced the wonder of recognizing myself and my husband and our parents and siblings in a baby's bright eyes or long limbs or stubby fingers.

But Jay and I *have* experienced the profound joy of loving children. We have been blessed as we have rocked other mothers' babies to sleep and befriended toddlers and teenagers. God has given us opportunities to make the children in our church feel important and valued. And we have been privileged to volunteer for the most selfless task of love on earth: parenthood.

HEAVEN'S FAMILY PLANNING

Psalm 68:6 says that "God sets the lonely in families." No matter how children come into a family, God's design is at work. And when children don't come, this is also God's design. When it doesn't look that way, it's only because we cannot always see heaven's true perspective from earth's vantage point. We rarely glimpse even fragments of the whole fantastic tableau of beautiful patterns God is weaving through time and space.

When Jay and I married at twenty (Linda) and twenty-two (Jay), we had, of course, planned our entire lives. We didn't want children. We didn't want pets. Two people who don't want babies or puppies deserve each other, don't they? But after a while, I changed my mind. I "gently" prodded Jay to reconsider, saying something like "Give me children lest I die!" He agreed, and we proceeded to "put in our order" by praying for a little girl. Each time we thought I might be pregnant, Jay and I would stare each other down (a favorite conflict-resolution technique for the very immature) while arguing about whether she would be named Autumn, my favorite girl's name, or Amanda, Jay's favorite.

We tried. Nothing happened. For ten years we tried. God did not appear to be on the job. He failed to fulfill our "order." We went to the complaint department, all to no avail. Then we went to plan B, which is usually God's plan A. We pursued adoption, feeling strongly that we were to apply not for an infant but for a sibling group of older children. We underwent examinations, investigations, and interrogations until Los Angeles County Adoptions decided we were probably "safe" and approved our request for a sibling group of up to four children—all six years of age or older.

Our wise social worker prepared us by reminding us of something important about love. She looked into our dreamy faces and starry eyes and said, "You say you'll love them and that will be enough. Well, love is hard work. Very hard work. Love is commitment. A high percentage of older-child adoptions fail. We'll see if you can love them enough." We gulped and renewed our commitment.

Since there are many sibling groups waiting for adoption across the country, we prayed for God's will in putting our family together. Soon we received a call from our social worker. "We have a sibling group we'd like you to consider, even though they don't fit your age parameters. The mother relinquished them and requested a Christian family who would be willing to meet with her before the adoption. You're the only ones who came up on the computer meeting both those criteria. There are only two children in this group and they are three and five years old. Will you consider them?"

"Well, sure, tell us more about them."

"They're both girls, green-eyed blondes. The five-year-

old's name is Autumn. The three-year-old's name is Amanda."
God had answered both our prayers!

When we met with the girls' birth mother, we learned
their middle names. Autumn's middle name is the same as mine,
Marie. And Amanda's middle name is Linn, the name my friends
and family have called me since my teenage years when I rebelled
against my "too-common" given name, Linda. God allowed us to
name our children even though at the time we were not even aware
of their births. While I was crying over my barrenness, another
woman was carrying my babies and giving them birth. While I was
feeling as if God were silent and uncaring, he was at work in his
own magnificent way.

Still young and foolish, we continued our attempts at
planning our own lives and felt in complete control of whether or
not we would have more children. After all, we were both infertile.
How in control of family planning can two parents be? Autumn
and Amanda kept us plenty busy, so we felt complete with the
national average of two kids.

After about five years we finally decided it was safe to leave
them with a baby-sitter during a pastors luncheon nearby. Jay was
at a conference, so I attended the monthly event with friends.
While there, I had an interesting encounter. A pastor I had never
met before approached me and tentatively said, "I know this is
strange, but I feel the Lord wants me to tell you something: 'Tell
her not to be afraid to have more children.'"

I smiled at the well-intentioned man and laughingly
replied, "Thank you, but I'm not afraid, because I'm not going to
have any more children." Noting my attitude, he asked if he could
pray for me, and I agreed. During his prayer he proclaimed that
the Lord would make our home an example of nurturing love and
that we would have a son who would grow up and accomplish many
specific things. When he was finished, he seemed quite pleased
with the whole thing, while I went home deeply disturbed. I
fervently hoped that what this pastor thought was from the Lord
was really something from his own imagination. But I also worried
about becoming pregnant at my "advanced" age—not quite Sarah's

age when she bore Isaac but getting up there. It was a little late to be enjoying a "blessed event."

Jay and I had just managed to put the unnerving encounter out of our thoughts when a visiting speaker came to our church. As we prayed together before the service, she suddenly got excited and said, "Oh, this is from the Lord! You're going to have more children. You're going to have a boy. He's going to do specific things. But don't be afraid, this will bring happiness into your home, and the Lord will make your home an example of nurturing love."

I shook my head, thinking, *No, no! I'm doomed!* This woman had just met us. She didn't know the other minister who had said the same things to me. This had to be from God. He knew we needed a lot of help accepting this detour in our family planning.

Jay and I decided that if this was God's plan, we didn't have to do anything to help it along. We went about our lives as usual. We thought we had it figured out. We didn't even recognize the fulfillment of the promise till long after God brought a special delivery to our home on Christmas Eve, just a month after the second "message from heaven."

We usually hold a Christmas open house at our home in early December. That year we decided to hold it on Christmas Eve in order to provide a special holiday for our single friends. One of our church members brought a coworker and her coworker's niece, Alex, a six-year-old pixie. Alex refused to stay in the kids' party room and wandered about the house getting into everything. Finally she cuddled into Jay's lap and settled down. For some reason he told her that she was so cute, he wished she could be his little girl, a thought that delighted her since Jay resembles Santa Claus in appearance and spirit. We didn't know then that Alex was also delighted because both her mom and dad had gone to jail a few months before. Her aunt had plenty of her own problems and didn't plan to keep her.

Alex's aunt discovered that we had adopted children before. Hoping we would fall in love with her niece, she made arrangements for Alex to spend weekends with us so she could attend Sunday school. We soon learned that Alex also had a little brother, Stephen, who had been separated from his mother, father, and sister and sat rocking numbly, silently, in a three-year-old's version of depression in a foster-care facility in the next county.

God presented us with a choice and gave us the courage to make the best choice. I have to admit that Jay coaxed me into it. I was still waiting for the pregnancy I thought was coming. We decided to help reunite Alex and Stephen and applied for an emergency foster-care license. By February Alex and Stephen moved in and blended into our family immediately. We were thrilled with our little guests, for they lightened up our lives with love and laughter.

Eventually the children's birth mother visited, and after her second visit in our home she asked us to adopt her children. We arranged an open adoption, allowing two visits, at Christmas and in the summer, with their mother, whom we call their "first mom." It was only after the adoption was finalized that we stopped waiting for a pregnancy and realized that the expected guests had arrived. We hadn't thought we needed more children, but we did need them, desperately. They brought so much more love into our home. However, when I met up again with that minister who first spoke to me about having more children, I begged him not to deliver any more messages to me, lest more children be delivered soon after.

MORE CHILDREN, MORE LOVE

Now, with four children, Jay and I were certain our family was complete. But, no, God apparently decided that we had been faithful with few, so several years after Alex and Stephen's arrival, he blessed us with more.

My younger sister's family had experienced troubles for some time. It was beginning to look as if children's services would remove the children from their home. I began to talk to Jay about having our three nieces and nephew move in with us. The first night I broached this, Jay's answer was definite. "I'm so sorry, but no. We don't have the emotional or physical resources."

I couldn't bear to see the children left to the care of strangers, so I prayed and asked Jesus to "have a little talk" with Jay. The next night, when Jay and I discussed it again, he said, "I think we can take two of them." I smiled and prayed again. The following evening I didn't even need to bring up the subject, because as soon as Jay got home from work, he blurted out, "All right, we'll take all of them!" "All of them" meant that with the addition of those four, we would now be raising eight children, most of them teenagers. This requires the kind of bravery that can be fueled only by love.

Loving children is costly in every way. Loving many children requires that every brain cell be engaged at all times; it requires that we summon every ounce of strength we can muster until the end of each day; it requires that we requisition endless supplies of love to replenish those that keep running out. Our social worker was right. Love is hard work. It is a choice we make. It is a commitment we keep. Launching little lives often means that our grown-up goals must wait.

Loving children is costly in every way.

When my nieces and nephew came to live with us, I was directing a national ministry. I could do that with four children, all teenagers, but I could not work full-time with eight children, one of them only five years old. I had to make an immediate decision about the ministry I had founded and directed for eleven years. I loved my work and the people I served. I loved the interaction with other ministry leaders, the creativity, the sense of accomplishment, the affirmation. But it was not a simple choice between helping the people on our mailing list and helping our family. If numbers were all that mattered, many precious families would be casualties of the pursuit of public ministry. Jesus made his priorities clear when he related the story of the shepherd who left the ninety-nine sheep to go find the one who needed him most.

The day my nieces and nephew moved in, I sat down with my exhausted, discouraged fourteen-year-old niece, Ruth, and explained that she no longer had to take care of her younger siblings. Jay and I would be the parents now. She could be a kid again and just worry about "books, blemishes, and boys," the way other teenage girls do. My decision to cancel my speaking engagements for the next year felt like no sacrifice at all when Ruth fell into my lap weeping, saying, "Thank you, Linnie, thank you."

In a vulnerable moment like this one, children's needs are so obvious, so compelling. But those needs are present daily, whether children reveal their vast need for love and care or have learned to do without. All children have the need to be unconditionally loved, valued, and cared for, whether they are capable of expressing that need or not. All children need an adult who would not just die for them but would do the more difficult task of living for them.

I packed up my office and sent the fruits of my labors off to other ministries because God can equip anyone to run a ministry. I accepted a long-term assignment that only I could do. There are thousands of people with the knowledge and experience to do exactly what I was doing in ministry. All God had to do was add the burden and the calling. I was the one with the family background to give the children what they needed most. They now live with people who have known them all their lives and love them. It has been two years since I surrendered public ministry for the sake of these children. Where other people used to pay me to deliver a lecture, my teenagers would gladly pay me not to. But I have no regrets. Time proves the rightness of a loving decision.

LOVING CHILDREN AS GOD LOVES THEM

God *lavishes* love on his children. God's Word says: "How great is the love the Father has lavished on us, that we should be called children of God! And that is what we are!" (1 John 3:1). In the same way, we need to lavish love on the children in our lives.

Shortly after my nieces and nephew came to live with us, Rachel, who was ten at the time, starred as an angel in our church Christmas play. After each of her angelic appearances, she would fade off into the background as the narrator proclaimed, "And the angel of the Lord disappeared." The third time the narrator said this, I sensed the Holy Spirit impressing on me, "Linda, that is just what has happened to Rachel. Help our little angel reappear."

Though Rachel possessed incredible talents, she was the middle child and had often gone unnoticed in her family. The trauma she had suffered had taught her to "disappear" during times of discord, to say nothing, to try to be invisible, to never speak her mind. Often when I visited her home prior to her moving in with us, I needed to search for her, for she was always hiding quietly, learning to be inconspicuous. When we spoke, I tried, often unsuccessfully, to draw out her feelings and opinions.

Jay and I began to concentrate on Rachel during our prayer time. We looked for ways to make her feel special. We worked to draw her out and affirm her opinions and desires. Gradually the "little angel" began to reappear. Today Rachel gets plenty of attention, and not just because of her flaming red hair. She's an accomplished athlete, an award-winning writer full of feelings she is eager to express—and she's as opinionated as her aunt.

How many children like Rachel have "disappeared" in the darkness of a void of love? Let's find them and help them shine as they were meant to do. Even one loving adult can make such a difference in a child's life. I once heard Dr. Louis McBurney, a physician who has spent his life giving to others, tell about his favorite aunt. "I guess I lucked out in the self-esteem department because I had an aunt who thought I was just about the best thing invented since chocolate cake." Dr. McBurney's aunt lavished love on him as a youth and in doing so provided vast supplies for him to share with others later.

JESUS CARES HOW WE TREAT CHILDREN

I went shopping recently for a baby-shower gift and spent a great deal of time in a large children's clothing store. I was appalled at what I heard going on between young children and their care-givers. Grandmothers or moms or, in some cases, baby-sitters yelled at the children, yanked them about, or spoke with sarcasm, harshness, or irritated impatience. The delightful displays of children's clothing and sweet baby outfits presented a shocking contrast to the way children were actually being treated. Why make children look adorable and then treat them with something other than adoring affection?

Go out into your world and watch children at school, at the grocery store, in the neighborhood, at church. Do you observe the adults in their lives ministering tender words, reassuring smiles, quick embraces, thoughtful answers to their many questions? Or do you see children without seat belts in moving cars; children being snapped at, yelled at, and even sworn at? Do you see parents helping with homework and listening to child-size struggles or shushing them, shooing them away, and using the television as a baby-sitter? Is there really enough love in this world for children?

Once again, Jesus is the perfect example for us. How did Jesus treat children?

> One day some parents brought their children to Jesus so he could touch them and bless them, but the disciples told them not to bother him. But when Jesus saw what was happening, he was very displeased with his disciples. He said to them, "Let the children come to me. Don't stop them! For the Kingdom of God belongs to such as these. I assure you, anyone who doesn't have their kind of faith will never get into the Kingdom of God." Then he took the children into his arms and placed his hands on their heads and blessed them. (Mark 10:13-16, NLT)

Have you ever taken a child in your arms and blessed him or her? My littlest one and I sometimes play this game together:

"Lizzy," I say, "do you know how much I love you? I love you a million, patillion, zazillion, fafillion, kerpillion!"

"Well, I love you infinity," Lizzy replies.

"Well, I love you infinity plus infinity," I assert.

"Well, I love you infinity times infinity, plus six!"

"OK, you win. I just can't top that number! But do you know why I love you? Is it because you're so pretty?" She shakes her head no and smiles through the ritual. "Then is it because you're so smart?"

"No!"

"Is it because you're so much fun?"

"No!"

"Then why do I love you so much?"

"Because God made me and he let you love me."

Yes, this may be the most inane thing you have ever read, but for a young child, it's pure delight. A lot of adults would give anything to recall hearing their mom or dad exclaim, "I love you a kerpillion!"

If we gave children the place Jesus accorded them, there would be no lack of Sunday school teachers and nursery volunteers. Every child who wanted to be involved would be fully sponsored for camping trips and mission projects. Children from single-parent homes would have adult friends to take them on outings and bring some welcome relief to their weary parents. Children would be greeted at church with smiles, hugs, and conversations. Children would love church because church members love them. That's not always the way it is, though, is it?

I know Christians who show their pets more care and affection than they show young people. It may be true that God custom-designed dogs, cats, and other pets to provide companionship and unconditional love and affection. Well, dogs, anyway. Cats place a few conditions on their affection for us. I know this because we've changed our minds about not having pets, too. Still, Jesus didn't have anything to say about dogs and cats. He does have a few words for us about children:

> See that you do not look down on one of these little ones. For I tell you that their angels in heaven always see the face of my Father in heaven. (Matthew 18:10)

> Then he put a little child among them. Taking the child in his arms, he said to them, "Anyone who welcomes a little child like this on my behalf welcomes me, and

anyone who welcomes me welcomes my Father who sent
me." (Mark 9:36-37, NLT)

When the chief priests and the teachers of the law saw the
wonderful things he did and the children shouting in the
temple area, "Hosanna to the Son of David," they were
indignant.

"Do you hear what these children are saying?" they
asked him.

"Yes," replied Jesus, "have you never read, 'From the
lips of children and infants you have ordained praise'?"
(Matthew 21:15-16)

Nurturing children, holding them in high regard, and
treating them with respect are not the exclusive responsibilities of
parents, grandparents, aunts, and uncles. All Christians, single or
married, young or old, can make more room in their hearts to
nurture children. We need to pray that our love for children
increases. Do you know of a child who has no extended family
nearby? Maybe that child would love a volunteer grandparent.
Could you befriend neighborhood children or be a big brother
or big sister to a child in a single-parent home? Do you need to
reconnect with grandchildren, nieces, or nephews? You might
even consider becoming a foster parent. As you pray, God will
grant you opportunities and ideas for ways you can communicate
love, respect, and regard for the children and young people
around you.

What a difference an adult's kindness can make in the
heart of a child. In "The Whisper Test" (*Leadership Journal*, winter
1995), Mary Ann Bird writes:

> I grew up knowing I was different, and I hated it. I was
> born with a cleft palate, and when I started school, my
> classmates made it clear to me how I looked to others: a
> little girl with a misshapen lip, crooked nose, lopsided
> teeth, and garbled speech.
> When schoolmates asked, "What happened to your

lip?" I'd tell them I'd fallen and cut it on a piece of glass. Somehow it seemed more acceptable to have suffered an accident than to have been born different. I was convinced that no one outside my family could love me.

There was, however, a teacher in the second grade whom we all adored—Mrs. Leonard by name. She was short, round, happy—a sparkling lady.

Annually we had a hearing test. . . . Mrs. Leonard gave the test to everyone in the class, and finally it was my turn. I knew from past years that as we stood against the door and covered one ear, the teacher sitting at her desk would whisper something, and we would have to repeat it back— things like "The sky is blue" or "Do you have new shoes?" I waited there for those words that God must have put into her mouth, those seven words that changed my life. Mrs. Leonard said, in her whisper, "I wish you were my little girl." Small acts of love can make a great difference in a young life.

America's value system often sees children more as both- ers than blessings and grants little esteem to those who care for children. But the Bible's value system says, "Religion that God our Father accepts as pure and faultless is this: to look after orphans and widows in their distress and to keep oneself from being polluted by the world" (James 1:27). God's Word reminds us that those who tenderly love and serve children and young people reflect God's love in its truest light. To lavish love on a child is to improve the future. A little love can even change the face of eternity.

I asked my older children to help me make a list of what makes them feel loved. Here are some of their answers:

• Spend time together working, playing, resting.
• Tell them you love them with words.
• Show them physical affection, hugs and smiles.
• Provide for their needs.
• Listen to them.

- Discipline them.
- Pray for them.
- Pray with them.
- Forgive their failures.
- Teach them God's ways.
- Teach them about life.
- Spend time with each child individually.
- Respect their private space and private feelings.
- Help them pursue interests and talents.
- Sympathize when they fail or hurt.
- Protect them from needless pain.
- Comfort them through unavoidable pain.
- Speak encouraging words.
- Teach and expect a sense of responsibility.
- Model good manners.
- Teach problem solving.
- Make them feel welcome and comfortable in their own home.
- Make their friends feel welcome.
- Communicate their importance and value.
- Tell positive stories about them that become family "legends."
- Make what's important to them important to you.
- Attend their games, performances, and activities.
- Say no only when really necessary. Say yes often.
- When you have to say no, explain why.
- Be an advocate for them with teachers, coaches, and other authorities when needed.
- Write love notes.
- Give them your complete attention when they are speaking.
- Show thoughtfulness and consideration.
- As they grow, let go, a little at a time.
- Apologize when you are wrong.
- Affirm good values and behavior.
- Talk about their future with optimism.
- Help them find a path to fulfill near-impossible dreams.
- Consciously and conscientiously raise your children the way you would like to have been raised.

Young children and all who do not know our Lord have only
one way of knowing how loving God is. They look at us.
If there be any flaw in our love, if we fail them at any point,
we make it just so much harder for them to see, to know,
to apprehend, His love. Do not let us fail our children.
"Love through me, O love of God."
AMY CARMICHAEL, *The Edges of His Ways*

We were as gentle among you as a mother feeding and caring for her own children.
1 THESSALONIANS 2:7, NLT

*Dear Father, give me a nurturing heart. Help me to be
God's love all dressed up as an auntie, a teacher, a grandma,
a mother, a friend. Let me enjoy the privilege of loving a child
with affection, tenderness, mercy, kindness, and patience.
In Jesus' name, amen.*

seven

THE RESPONSIBILITY OF LOVE

loving with right priorities

Years ago when we had just four small children, they were play-acting on the back porch. Amanda, my little leader, laid out the rules. I could hear them through the kitchen window as I worked at my computer, answering correspondence for the ministry I directed. *Cute,* I thought. *They're playing house or maybe school.* But the rules were about secretaries, mailing lists, and catalogs. Amanda proclaimed herself the director, telling the others, "Go away now. I'm busy."

Hmmm . . . I called out to them, "Sweeties, what are you playing?"

"Nonprofit corporation!" they shouted. Nonprofit corporation? They can pronounce *nonprofit corporation?* And the director acts busy and self-important and shoos her children away? *Uh-oh.*

I took a coffee break to mull over what I'd just heard. Perhaps I had been spreading myself too thin—trying to balance the duties of a pastor's wife, mother of four, and director of a ministry to ministry families. I loved my work. Could it be possible that I was neglecting some area of my life? Or some area of four little lives?

That night I dreamed my children grew up and wrote a best-seller about me. The title: *Corporate Mommy Dearest.*

They went on the talk-show circuit. Oprah lined up a show with the theme "Pitiful Adult Children of Neglectful Christian Leaders with Mixed-Up Priorities." Leaning in for a misty-eyed close-up, she asked, "We've all seen your mother acting sweet on Christian television. Tell us what she was really like at home."

Alex began, "Well, she spoke to thousands about family life in the ministry. But we rarely saw her." Autumn defended me. "She was very affectionate. She always kissed us good-bye on her way to the airport."

The book spawned a movie. I grew hopeful as I saw the names of glamorous actresses appear in the opening credits. It turned out that they played my daughters. The actress portraying me? Roseanne. That's when I woke up.

I was determined to prevent publication of that book! Oh yes, and to win the love and affection of my precious darlings. I had grown up with the Pillsbury motto "Nothin' says lovin' like somethin' from the oven," so when the children came home from school that day, a homemade chocolate cake was waiting for them.

Stephen asked, "Mom, who is that for?"

"Someone very special," I replied.

"Oh, who's coming over?"

I smiled sweetly. "It's for you, dear."

"Oh, we get to eat with the company tonight?"

I served it immediately to avoid further interrogation.

That night my husband and I evaluated the situation. "Dear," I said, "how many more years will we have our beloved children here with us to train and love and influence their lives?"

"About ten more years. I hope."

"And, dear, how many more years do we have to develop our ministries?"

"Keep eating that leftover cake, and you'll have about two years."

"No, really."

"OK, about thirty."

After consulting the calculator, we saw that we needed to set some new priorities.

The first thing I did was remove my office from my home to a spare room at our church. (Being the wife of the pastor has advantages.) I came in to work during school hours. Home became home. Mommy became mommy. No more dining-room computer calling to me at all hours, "Come heeere. There's always more to dooo." I let go of some of my responsibilities at church. Other people actually volunteered to do those tasks. I had entered the realm of the miraculous.

I met with my nonprofit board. "Board," I said, "I can't do everything."

"We're glad you have attained enlightenment," they said. We made a plan to continue essential services and cut back on expansion.

Suddenly I had time to help with homework, sit and talk, do fun things as a family, drive kids to lessons and activities, and prepare meals consisting of food groups other than Pizza Group, Taco Group, and Chinese Take-Out Group.

The children began to come home with straight A's, never fought again, and vowed to grow up to become medical missionaries! OK, that was an exaggeration. But they were happier. They began doing better in school. Their spiritual lives developed. And they knew for sure that I loved and valued them. As for me, I had the luxurious satisfaction of knowing that I was right where I belonged.

Maybe someday my children really will grow up and write a book about me: *Mothering Heights* or *A Mom for All Seasons* or maybe *All I Really Needed to Know I Learned from My Mom*. I can dream, can't I?

THE CIRCLES OF LOVE

Love has priorities. God is a God of semblance and order. He knows that our hours, our energy, our emotional capabilities are finite. We can't love as he loves. We can't love everyone in our sphere of influence equally. We certainly can't treat everyone equally. Instead we move from one circle to another. It may help to picture a bull's-eye design of concentric circles. We are most likely to hit the mark when we aim for the innermost circles first. Let's take a look at the circles of love.

PRIORITY I: THE SACRED CIRCLE

The innermost circle is big enough for two—God and you. Jesus said, "If anyone comes to me and does not hate his father and mother, his wife and children, his brothers and sisters—yes, even his own life—he cannot be my disciple" (Luke 14:26). Jesus clearly loved his own family, his disciples, and his friends. But not with the devotion with which he loved God. Many other Bible passages counsel us to love our wives, husbands, and children, to care for our aging parents, and to love one another deeply.

It's clear from the context that Jesus is using hyperbole to ask the crowd that followed him to stop counting the miracles, healings, and blessings and instead to count the cost of following him. Our love for Jesus must be so profound that our love for our family and friends seems like hate in comparison.

In some situations we must make a choice that makes it seem as if we "hate" the ones we really love. For instance, when a young person is called to the mission field but family members beg her not to go, she must follow Christ, the one she loves the most.

Sometimes our loved ones won't understand the intensity and intimacy of our love relationship with Jesus. They won't understand how clearly we hear God's voice leading us. They won't be able to walk with us down the path where God leads. In those times there may be misunderstandings between us and our loved ones while they wait to see where we're going. God may be leading us on a lonely path where only he can be our guide and only he can hold our hand. In those times, even though the misunderstandings are painful, we must continue to follow Jesus.

This innermost circle is the source of all other loves.

Entering the Sacred Circle

Perhaps you are reading this book about the wonders of God's love and you have yet to experience that love for yourself. Many people seem open to a general belief in God but think of Jesus as simply a great teacher. Jesus was much more than that. His life and teaching are supported by more historical evidence and eyewitness accounts than the life of any other person of ancient history. The things he taught are radical and definite: "I am the way, the truth, and the life. No one can come to the Father except through me" (John 14:6, NLT).

For Jesus to make such a statement, one of two things must be true: Either he was a pompous delusionary, or he really was the Son of God and the only way to find acceptance with God. We cannot know God without accepting him in the image of his Son. Are you a friend of God? Jesus came to suffer for our sins, to wear a crown of thorns, to die so that we could wear the crown of life. He rose from the dead and will show himself real to any sincere inquirer. Do you know that your sins have been forgiven? Are you getting to know Jesus and experiencing a dynamic relationship with him? If not, tell God that you want to know him deeply and personally. Jesus is the lover and redeemer of our souls. Ask him to forgive your sins and accept you into his family. Once you have done that, you need to find a church that is characterized by the love of God. People there can help you get started reading and studying the Bible to learn more about God and his great love for you.

If you already have a rich relationship with Jesus, follow the instructions that Mary, Jesus' mother, gave the servants at the wedding feast at Cana: "Do whatever he tells you" (John 2:5, NLT). This is good advice for our daily lives. We need do only what God asks of us. The apostle Paul said, "I can do everything with the help of Christ who gives me the strength I need" (Philippians 4:13, NLT). We can't do everything, but we *can* do everything God asks us to do.

We can't do everything, but we *can* do everything God asks us to do.

Love for God is the first commandment. Love for God is paramount. All other loving relationships stand outside this sacred circle.

PRIORITY 2: YOU

God's Word tells us to love our neighbors as ourselves (Mark 12:31). I like to paraphrase this as "Love your neighbor *and* yourself." Everyone would agree that God wants us to love our neighbors. Why is it so hard to love ourselves that way? If you don't take care of yourself, your physical body, your emotions and intellect, and especially your heart and soul, you'll have no overflow of love to give to others. When we are sick and tired from overwork or lack of care for our bodies, we are hardly vibrant examples of abundant life in Christ.

How can you be careful to love yourself? Consider who you would be if you suddenly found yourself laid off at work or widowed or facing an "empty nest." If you suddenly were not an executive or suddenly not a spouse or suddenly not a parent, would you know who you are? Are you nurturing other parts of yourself, the parts that always wanted to earn a college degree or begin a different career or learn horsemanship or develop your artistic side?

Many excel at caring for externals but neglect their spiritual lives. Take good loving care of your soul. Feed it the Word of God. Nurture it in prayer. Connect with other Christians in a local church. Develop relationships with people who will hold you accountable. It makes sense to care most for that part of you that is eternal—your soul.

Only you can make the choice to take good, loving care of yourself. You alone decide whether or not to exercise, to turn off the TV and get more sleep, to eat sensibly, to control your temper and all other factors that contribute to or destroy your health.

Part of our motivation for taking care of ourselves is our loving concern for others. We can't fully express a life of love without taking care of ourselves. If we are married, we want our spouses to continue to be attracted to us, so we eat carefully and exercise. If we are parents, we want to live to see our children graduate, so we keep them in mind when the struggle to quit smoking becomes excruciatingly difficult. If we are single and working or going to school, we do all we can to take care of ourselves so that we have the energy to invest lovingly in the lives of others. Living and loving here on earth requires a body. Take care of yours! Grow in love and appreciation for the unique personality you are.

PRIORITY 3: YOUR SPOUSE

I felt so sorry for the nice man. While waiting in line at a health food store, I overheard him, in a gentle and pleasant manner, ask his wife if she wouldn't like to try a new product on display. She snarled back in disdain, not at the product, but at him, "You're so ridiculous! I told you we don't need anything more!"

He seemed accustomed to her abusive tone. Unfazed, he replied, "Well, this looked like something you'd like."

"Well, it's not!" she growled. "Just get in line, will you?!"

I did not want to embarrass the man further by even looking at them, but I wished I could say to his wife, "If you don't want to love him, I'm sure someone else would be happy to give it a try."

If you are married, do you remember your vows to love, honor, and cherish till death do you part? Vows to love in the bloom of youth, in the withering of old age, and during all the trips to the grocery store in between? We could all speak more kindly, wait more patiently, say yes more often. We could all love our spouses more tenderly.

We never really know in the beginning what a marriage will entail. But we can trust that Jesus' love is enough love to see us through. Maybe our toughest challenge is trying to love our honey no matter how he replaces the empty toilet-paper roll (or doesn't) or how he squeezes the toothpaste from the tube. Other couples face tremendous challenges: a partner's paralyzing accident, lengthy unemployment, recovery from infidelity, the death of a child, debilitating illness.

In *A Promise Kept: The Story of an Unforgettable Love* (Tyndale House, 1998), Robertson McQuilkin told readers about life with his wife, Muriel, who suffered from early-onset Alzheimer's disease. To provide full-time care, he decided to step down as president of South Carolina's Columbia Bible College and Seminary (now Columbia International University) and nurture her through her long illness. He accomplished this with tender love and quiet joy. He writes: "Love is said to evaporate if the relationship is not mutual, if it's not physical, if the other person doesn't communicate, or if one party doesn't carry his or her share of the load. When I hear the litany of essentials for a happy marriage, I count off what my beloved can no longer contribute, and I contemplate how truly mysterious love is." Godly love flourishes, even through the most severe trials of life.

PRIORITY 4: YOUR CHILDREN

Be the best parent you can be. If your children have only one parent actively involved in their lives, it is even more important to grant priority to this love relationship. Teach your children about the Savior, read God's Word to them, read books on parenting, go to classes, work diligently to meet your children's physical, emotional, and spiritual needs. You are the most important person in your child's world. Children will return all the love you can give them—while they're young, anyway, and then beginning again sometime in their twenties. Between those times, we need to love our teenagers patiently and not believe it when they say they hate us. They will grow up. In the meantime, make a generous investment. It will be repaid many times over.

The way we love our children evolves over time. Love paints a different portrait at every age and every stage. But the love and support of a parent is of supreme value at every age. In "Insider Turned Out," an article by Edward Gilbreath (*Christianity Today*, February 1996), former Southern Baptist Convention president Jimmy Allen talks about his son, who is gay:

> We've known that Skip is HIV positive for about seven years. He now has full-blown AIDS. . . . Skip and I have a very warm, personal, loving relationship. We've learned to move beyond theology to love. We've had to deal with each other. He wanted approval of his behavior, and I could only offer him love and acceptance. We have vast differences of opinion, but that has not stopped our love. . . . Compassion always reaches beyond barricades and barriers to get to where need is.

Loving a child through youth to adulthood, and sometimes into eternity ahead of the parent, is a sacred trust, a task of love for which there is no substitute.

PRIORITY 5: YOUR PARENTS

Parents are important people throughout our lives. The Bible instructs us to care for them in their old age (1 Timothy 5:4). Honor them with love and attention. Try to see them at least once a year if you live far apart. Don't rob your children of a relationship with their grandparents. This relationship may require intense caregiving on your part in your parents' older years.

Whatever age you are, the way you treat your parents speaks volumes about the status of your relationship with God. In some ways we can see it as a barometer of our spiritual life. As young people we owe them respect, allegiance, and obedience. Yes, it's our job to become mature, separate individuals by the time we've reached young adulthood. But we still need to be loving and respectful as we become those "separate" individuals. As adults, we owe our parents the same unconditional love we desire from them.

PRIORITY 6: YOUR EXTENDED FAMILY

How much time do we give to our relationship with our extended family? Aunts and uncles, adult brothers and sisters, grandparents, and nieces and nephews are all important to our lives. Pray for all of them, and give as much love as possible.

The role of a grandparent or aunt or uncle offers one of the greatest opportunities to show love. In those roles we are in a position to exude near adoration of the young objects of our affection. Kids need significant nonparent adults in their lives, adults who have the fun of bestowing love and attention without feeling the need to be a disciplinarian. For children, this kind of relationship is bliss!

Many times we are tempted to neglect grandkids or nieces or nephews as they enter their awkward teenage years. It can be difficult to communicate with a young person who only grunts in response to your questions or seems to work at looking bored when you're together. But now is the time to find creative new ways to communicate love for them. Try letters, E-mail messages, brief phone calls, small rewards for good grades. Keep hugging and saying, "I love you." They may not cuddle up to you the way they did when they were younger, but your expressions of love and acceptance are still important to them.

PRIORITY 7: YOUR BROTHERS AND SISTERS IN CHRIST

"Whenever we have the opportunity, we should do good to everyone, especially to our Christian brothers and sisters" (Galatians 6:10, NLT). Sometimes our church family can feel even closer and more significant to us than our relatives. As members of the family of God we can and should enjoy those relationships that provide mutual understanding of the Lord and his ways. We can be ready to extend hospitality and help when others need them. We can help to carry others' burdens, support our spiritual brothers and sisters in prayer, and find ways to encourage them. And, of course, we can always look for ways to spend time together just enjoying the friendship of other believers.

PRIORITY 8: MORE CIRCLES

After looking at all the priorities above, it might seem at first glance that we've covered pretty much everyone. But there are others who may or may not be included in the circles we've looked at, people we talk to or spend time with on a regular, even daily, basis. So who else should we be including? Here are some additional circles of love:

Love your friends. A friend is a treasure. Nurture your friendships. Take an afternoon a week to keep up through phone calls, letters, or "doing lunch" with a friend nearby. Like so many things in life, friendships break down from neglect. Only the ones we work at maintaining survive. Friendship is not only a present blessing, it is an investment in our future. Robertson McQuilkin, who knows firsthand how friendship can sustain us in the trials of old age, says, "Those who don't build friendships in the spring and summer of life must find winter a lonely time" ("Muriel's Blessing," *Christianity Today,* February 5, 1996).

Love your neighbors. We gain good neighbors by being good neighbors ourselves. Take "prayer walks" through your neighborhood, and look for opportunities to help and be friendly. Keep up your home and yard. You might even consider raking your neighbor's yard while you're at it. Kind deeds and gracious greetings make good neighbors.

Like so many things in life, friendships break down from neglect. Only the ones we work at maintaining survive.

Give back love to those who have invested in your life. Can you recall a kind-hearted teacher who helped you master your worst subject? Look her up and say thank you. Or drop a note, telling her how she made a difference in your life. Are you missing a childhood friend who moved away years ago? Perhaps you can reconnect. Think back to those whose love and thoughtfulness affected the course of your life, and let them know how their investment of love has paid dividends.

Love your coworkers. If you asked for a job and they hired you, you have a major responsibility to fulfill. Your testimony for Christ depends on your faithfulness on the job. If you don't love your work, pray, do research, and find a career path that you would find more fulfilling and enjoyable. If you work outside the home, time in the workplace takes a third of each day and most of your waking hours. Spend that time doing something you love, with people you love. Respect and honor your boss and coworkers. Live considerately with them. When you get up for coffee, offer to get some for your secretary, as well. Live in humility as a citizen of the kingdom of heaven, even at work. Remember birthdays, Secretary's Day, Boss's Day, and the like, and celebrate finished projects, raises, promotions, new clients, birthdays, and other milestones.

Love strangers. After taking time for all the above, there still may be room to minister to those we don't even know through service, prayer, outreach, witness, or giving. This is what most of us think of as ministry. But we should approach these opportunities only after we tend our own "mission field" consisting of all of the other relationships listed above.

Finally, love your enemies. Loving your enemies is an act of forgiveness and graciousness and usually requires supernatural empowerment. Love them by praying for them, blessing them, and treating them with dignity. Refrain from speaking ill of them. Do good to them when the opportunity arises. Our love for others is not at all dependent on their love for us.

WHOM DO YOU LOVE?

I believe we will answer to the Lord concerning our treatment of those God has loaned us to love. When we appear before the Father to give an account concerning those he gave us to love, will those people be in better condition than when we received them? Or will they be damaged from neglect or abuse? It would be a shameful thing to have to return a formerly bright and shiny object of God's love back to him, all worn out and broken from mistreatment by our own hands. While learning to love your spouse or your children or any others in your circles of influence, keep in mind who made them and who is watching over them.

This book is simply an encouragement to grow in love. It cannot possibly delineate all the ways to nurture a marriage, raise children, be a good friend, or minister to others through love. Your local Christian bookstore offers books, videos, and other treasures of wisdom to help you learn to love more deeply and diligently in all of your relationships. Local churches and parachurch organizations offer seminars and conferences. There are newsletters, radio programs, and many other sources of instruction for strengthening all our relationships. A person for whom love is a priority will pursue these avenues of learning about commitment and effectiveness in key relationships. Which of your relationships needs insight and answers? Take advantage of the in-depth instruction and advice available through so many wise authors, speakers, and leaders.

Whom has God given you to love? Chart out your own circles of love, naming the people who belong in each concentric circle. Look for circles where there's still room for growth. Perhaps you'd like to make more friends or get to know more of your neighbors. Perhaps you've neglected relatives who were your sun and moon in your younger years. Reconnect!

Do you appropriately spend most of your devotion, time, and effort on those in the innermost circles? Do you give your own needs any attention at all? As you look at your circles, you may notice that you spend more time with coworkers or friends when your family would like more of your attention. Perhaps God isn't really in the center of your life. Make the needed adjustments, and watch your circles of love expand.

WHEN LOVES COLLIDE

When we are following God's call to love, we may encounter conflicts of interest. Sometimes when choices conflict, the damage in the collision will be minor or nonexistent. At other times a conflict of interest can have enormous impact on many or intense impact on a few, affecting their entire lives even into eternity. At those times, we must weigh our choices on the balance of love with great precision. Such decisions call for careful assessment, wise counsel, and prayer that continues until we hear a definite answer.

My husband, Jay, loves the country of India and its people so much that he wants to be buried there when he dies. Our church supports many ministries in India, including Bible colleges, churches, leper homes, and several orphanages. Jay tries to travel to India for a month each year on a short-term missions trip. He takes one of our children and a delegation of others from our church. He also takes small toys and items of play jewelry and candy for the children in the orphanages. He also tries to bring one or two of the orphans back with him, but so far I've held my ground and pleaded that we seem to be full for now.

When all of our children reached their teen years and Jay began to plan his next trip overseas, I asked him to consider not going for a while. Even though one child would get to go with him and have a special experience with Dad, all of the children seemed to need us both more than ever once they were in their teen years. So Jay postponed a trip to the India he loves for the priority of loving his family. I hope he will go again after we have an emptier nest at home.

Only Jesus can be with everyone he loves at once and see to all of our needs at the same time. We all encounter everyday conflicts of interest because we have limited time and energy. Maybe your roommate would like you to attend an awards presentation at her office, but your sister is in town on an infrequent visit that same night. Or three different grandchildren have Saturday games, and you are invited to all of them. Or you're in debt, but you feel drawn to support a local ministry. Perhaps your husband wants more time with you, but you love your volunteer work. How do you choose?

Here are some guidelines for avoiding an accident when love is on a collision course:

Be Wholly Devoted to God

The first commandment always comes first: Love God supremely. If your fiancé wants to engage in premarital sex because "we're almost married anyway," you put your love for God far ahead of your desire to please your fiancé. Jesus said, "If you love me, you will obey what I command" (John 14:15). Breaking God's laws is never an act of love toward God or toward another person.

It's important to know and obey God's Word. Never allow an illegitimate "love" to grow in your heart. "Love" (or more accurately, desire) for your friend's spouse or for an unbeliever if you are a Christian is not a love that God will bless, for he cannot deny his own Word, and he has already spoken on the subject. When you start driving the wrong way on a one-way street, you can expect injuries or even fatalities when the inevitable collision occurs. The God of love made loving laws and precepts for our good. Read the Word of God. Memorize it. Meditate on it. Let God's Word guide you.

Consult Others Who May Be Affected

Rarely do our decisions affect only one or two people. They may involve your roommates, your coworkers, or your family. Discuss the issues involved. You all may decide to sacrifice together to show love to neighbors or even strangers. My family chose to allow me to go on retreat with my computer for a few weeks to write this book. They excused me from my daily obligations of love to them for a time so that I could devote my time completely to the writing project. Love is flexible and adaptable. It yields to others when the need arises.

A common collision occurs around the Christmas holidays. A single adult from a family that suffered divorce must decide if she will spend Christmas with Mom's family or with Dad's family. Or a young couple must choose between Thanksgiving invitations extended by both sets of parents. Discuss the options with all concerned, and come up with something as equitable and loving as possible. Even if someone ends up being disappointed, the effort you made to discuss the issue and be sensitive to others' feelings will alleviate some of the inevitable disappointment. All people really want to know is, "Do you care about me?" If you care enough to explain and to listen, mutual understanding may soften the disappointment.

Find a Compromise That Doesn't Compromise Your Values

Jay and I both frequently travel and speak. As our children grew older, we were concerned that they might view ministry as something that was always taking a parent away from them. So both Jay and I decided to include one or two children on our speaking trips. Our children have traveled all over the country, sightseeing and also seeing exactly what Mom and Dad do in ministry. After we made this decision, our speaking ministry became an exciting opportunity for our children instead of just another deprivation.

Of course, sometimes there can be no compromise. A friend's mother was angry with her sister over a petty mishap and wanted to exclude her from my friend's wedding invitation list. My friend said, "I'm sorry, Mom, but I love my aunt and will continue to see her and invite her to family celebrations. You need to resolve your problems with her before it's too late." Her mother was angry, but both women attended the wedding, and they later reconciled. We may temporarily lose the approval of some people by lovingly standing up for what is right, but ultimately our actions will encourage and model real love to everyone involved. When you suffer for doing right, comfort yourself with the reminder that you have the approval that matters most—the approval of God.

Pray

When you are not at peace about a decision that you must make, pray before you cast the deciding vote. Then, wait expectantly for God's guidance. He has answers we can't imagine. Jesus says that his sheep know his voice. After following him for a while, you will recognize his voice, too. If you think you've never heard it before, just recall a time when you were about to do something totally contrary to God's leading and you heard an inner *no!* loud and clear. Many of us have had that experience. But we can also learn to "hear" the quiet affirmations and instructions God longs to give us. God does care about even the smallest decision. First Peter 5:7 says: "Give all your worries and cares to God, for he cares about what happens to you" (NLT). God is pleased when we acknowledge our dependence on him, and he desires to lead us. Begin to trust that still small voice of reassurance that guides us gently and faithfully. We must learn to discern his voice if we are to follow his leading.

It will be easier for our loved ones to overlook the inevitable slights, disappointments, and even occasional offenses or deep wounds we cause if our good intentions and persistent efforts to love are easily recognizable. Let everyone see that you are doing your best to love each person in your circles of love.

> The real test of my loving is not that I feel loving, but the other person feels loved by me.
> MORTON T. KELSEY, *Companions on the Inner Way*

> *We are taking pains to do what is right, not only in the eyes of the Lord but also in the eyes of men.*
> 2 CORINTHIANS 8:21

Dear Lord, increase my ability and my opportunities to love. Help me to follow your priorities as I love those you place in my life. Make my life a life of symmetry and balance. And help me to hear your voice and follow your loving instructions. In the name of Jesus, amen.

eight

DILIGENT LOVE

loving our families with eternity in mind

Some of us tend to think that surely our family would win first
prize in a national competition for dysfunctional family of the
year. Then we listen to our friends' stories and feel thankful for
the way we grew up. One friend recently called to share her pain.
She said that her brother was in jail, her sister was abusing her
sons, and her in-laws were attacking and rejecting her. My friend's
strength was spent in weeping and worry. While trying to care for
her own family, she also carried a heavy burden of distress from
her extended family. She felt exhausted, frustrated, lonely, and
overwhelmed. We can escape difficult neighbors and coworkers by
moving or changing jobs. But our families are our families for the
rest of our lives. How do we persevere in love when it hurts so
much and is so costly?

   The distress of severe family dysfunction is increasingly
common. Family members or grown children who can't handle
life on their own can raise our emotional stress to staggering
levels. Even if societal and familial dysfunction were not issues,
we all struggle with sin on a daily basis, and the consequences of
sin are painful for both sinners and their loved ones. How can we
function as loving and joyful servants of our Lord and others when
we feel immobilized by pain and disappointment with our parents,
our siblings, our children, or others close to us?

WHEN THE PAIN IS CRUSHING

There are times when our emotional pain is so intense that we can't deal with the problems on our own. If you feel emotionally crushed, think about getting professional help. Talk to a pastor or a Christian counselor who can help you to sort out the issues and find ways of working through the difficulties or of coping when there is no immediate solution. Reading books on codependency can help us to sort out whether we are trying to help others because they have a legitimate need or because we "need to be needed." There is a vast difference between offering appropriate assistance and feeling the need to control someone else's life. If your relationship with a relative is making your life miserable, it may be time to take a look at the emotional patterns involved.

Even when a burden is yours to share, distribute the weight. Ask others to help carry the burden in prayer. I've found it helpful to "trade" prayer lists. I pray for a friend's family, and she prays for mine. The great sufferer Job found help when he took his eyes off of his own plight, focused on God, and prayed for his friends (Job 42:10).

Every burden ultimately belongs to the Lord. Cast your burdens on him, and he will sustain you. Rest in the assurance that he is with you (even when it feels as if he is far away) and promises to make your burden light by sharing the load.

WHEN YOUR FAMILY PAST IS PAINFUL

Trust God with your past as well as your future. We don't know all our needs, but God does, and even though it may be hard to understand, he places each of us in our families for a purpose. Does this mean it was God's will for your mom to be an alcoholic or your parents to divorce? No, but it does mean that you may have received a measure of grace that others did not require and so have grown from the experience. God can use your past to prepare you to comfort and bring healing to others in similar circumstances. There are important and positive things about your character and personality and the gifts God has given you that would not be there had you grown up in different circumstances. In *Letters of C. S. Lewis,* Lewis writes: "God, who foresaw your tribulation, has specially armed you to go through it, not without pain but without stain."

Trust God with your past as well as your future.

Ask God to redeem *all* of your experiences. God uses everything, even our family's faults, to shape us. God has no junkyard. Everything we turn over to him becomes 100 percent recyclable, redeemable, and useful in our lives and the lives of others.

REFRAIN FROM JUDGING

Many of us don't really know how our parents grew up and what forces shaped their parenting style. Trying to understand them in the context of their entire lives can prove helpful. Your mom was also a daughter. Maybe what she provided for you was a feast of love compared to the scraps she grew up with. She may have really struggled to do her best. There are things about your parents that you don't know—and maybe shouldn't know.

Remember that while we may be parents or siblings or children here, from God's perspective, all of us are dearly loved children. And all of us will give an account to him about how we spent our lives and how we treated the people in them. We will be judged with the same measure we use to judge others. Do you really want your children to be as hard on you as you are on your parents? Love each other, accept each other, try to understand each other, look for the best and appreciate the good in each other, and you'll have a more gracious yardstick to measure up to with your own kids and with God.

LOVE AND ACCEPT YOUR FAMILY

The apostle Paul wrote: "*If it is possible, as far as it depends on you,* live at peace with everyone" (Romans 12:18, italics added). We need to work toward that goal every day. But sometimes living at peace with another person is just not possible. I have a friend whose mother steals from her and maligns her. Others have fathers who abused them and have refused to accept responsibility for what they have done. People who find themselves in situations such as these may need to sever ties with some of their family members. When that is the case, the only honor you can offer your parents or others is to pray for them. You need not expose yourself to further abuse by anyone who is emotionally or physically threatening to your children or yourself. But most of us are dealing with occasional hurts and frustrations or perhaps ongoing grief about foolish choices family members have made. In these cases, we need to forgive, accept, and love our families just the way they are.

Tolstoy wrote that when you love someone, you love the whole person, just as he or she is, not as you would like that person to be. When visiting relatives who are not Christians, I may pray in anguish over their souls at night, but during the day I go picnicking, berry picking, hiking, and splashing in swimming holes with them as if I hadn't a care in the world. My burdens belong to the Lord, not to everyone around me. We can miss out on wonderful times with our loved ones if we withhold our affection or our involvement with them just because they do not follow Jesus. Enjoy spending time with your loved ones who are not yet followers of Jesus. Appreciate all that is good about them. God can enrich our lives through our relationships with them.

HELP YOUR FAMILY TO LOVE AND ACCEPT YOU

It's easy for us to feel as if we are always having to exercise patience toward family members who may not be Christians, but we need to remember that they may also be exercising patience toward us. Coming to know Christ doesn't instantly smooth out all of our rough edges and make us easy to live with. We will be striving till the day we die to conform to the image of Christ.

Try to recall how you felt about Christians before you were one. I remember that I was wary of them, for they imposed their views with a surety that seemed pompous. Because Christians believe so strongly in the truth of God's Word, we can seem like inflexible know-it-alls. The fact that we may choose not to participate in some activities and entertainments can make us seem like snobs or prudes. To non-Christians, the way we live out the Christian life can appear ridiculous rather than inviting.

Ask the Lord to help you relate to your family members in an authentic, down-to-earth way, sharing your whole life with them, both the victories and the struggles. Once, as a young Christian, my husband shared a painful struggle with his mother, who was not yet a believer. She said, "Thank you. I really appreciate you telling me that. Ever since you became a Christian, it seemed you were trying to appear perfect. I'm glad to know you're still human." His vulnerability helped build a bridge toward greater understanding.

Some family members may still be offended at times, no matter how sincerely we love them and try to do our best by them. Jesus is an offense to those who refuse him. But we needn't add to that offense by speaking or acting insensitively. Ask God to help you love those in your family and to express love in such a way that they feel respected, accepted, and valued. Learn from your relatives, honor them, value them, appreciate and affirm them. And humbly ask for forgiveness when you find that you have offended them.

ASK GOD TO HEAL YOU OF INNER PAIN

When my older brother, Danny, died, I experienced immobilizing grief for weeks. I knew that as a young man he had accepted Christ as his Savior. God also gave him several days in the hospital to prepare for death. But even though I felt assured of our future reunion in heaven, I was still stunned by the loss. Finally I set a few days aside to grieve and pray. I wrestled with God out loud for several hours, pleading that I really could not carry the intense level of grief I felt concerning not only my brother's death but also his tormented life. I begged God to touch my heart and heal me. After a few hours, I began to feel God's healing touch in my heart.

That night I had a vivid dream that also helped me resolve my feelings about my brother and let him go. I dreamed I was in San Francisco again and saw Danny on the street. I ran to him and clung to him, so thrilled that he had not died after all. But as I held him, I saw that he was still mentally ill, his life still so difficult, confusing, and lonely. Then the dream changed, and I saw Danny as he was dying and then his first moments in heaven as

Jesus greeted him and held him in his arms, safe at last. Once again I saw him in San Francisco, not having obtained that blessed deliverance! My grief at seeing that was greater than my grief over his death. I was filled with sadness that he was not yet safe in heaven.

That dream showed me what a great and loving gift Danny's early death was to him. Of course it is better to be with Jesus and be whole than to suffer here. God answered my prayer for resolution with a healing touch and a dream of explanation. Since then, I've been able to think about Danny with peace and even thankfulness for both his life and his death.

There are many things in our lives that cause incredible inner turmoil and nearly incurable sorrow and grief. No amount of counseling or Bible reading even begins to alleviate the pain. For these things, too, Jesus died and took all of our pain on himself. I have experienced and witnessed both physical and emotional healing from God. Ask him boldly for heavenly help, and see him heal what no one and nothing else can.

WHEN FAMILY MEMBERS NEED ASSISTANCE

In Paul's letter to the Galatians he gives two directives that seem to be contradictory: "Carry each other's burdens, and in this way you will fulfill the law of Christ" (Galatians 6:2) and "Each one should carry his own load" (Galatians 6:5). Paul urges his readers to grow in responsibility and strength so that they will not be a burden to anyone else. But from time to time all of us have burdens that are too heavy for us to carry alone. If you see a brother or sister in temporary need or legitimate long-term need (widows and orphans, single parents, or those who are chronically ill, for instance), help them yourself, and look for other sources of appropriate support, both practical and emotional. If you are caring for a relative with long-term illness, take advantage of all the practical resources available, such as respite care. Attend a support group to help you cope with the emotional issues involved. And find a prayer group or prayer partner who will support you in praying for the spiritual resources you'll need.

HEALTHY HELP

It can be difficult for us to determine on a case-by-case basis what would help someone the most, both now and long-term. Once, when a relative was upset, I listened to her and then replied, "Well, I could respond in a way that would make you feel better this afternoon. Or I could say some things that could help you feel better in your future but won't feel very good to you right now. Which would you rather hear?" She chose the latter, and I was able to say some difficult but constructive things to her. We both would have been more comfortable with the usual tea and sympathy. And sometimes that is the best way to help—a cup of tea and a listening ear, maybe a shoulder to cry on as someone shares a deep burden. But that wasn't what my relative really needed this time. At other times she has needed help to pay her rent, buy groceries, or clean her home. At those times it's not enough to offer words, telling people how to dig themselves out of their self-pity. We must be willing to roll up our sleeves, dig in, and come alongside with practical help.

Sometimes, even though we have the best of intentions, we hurt others by "helping" those who can and should learn to care for themselves. Caring for an elderly parent or a just-divorced brother is part of our responsibility as loving family members. But other things are not our responsibility: giving financial support to those who are criminals, addicts unwilling to get help, or the chronically lazy is not helpful. God lovingly provides consequences for wrong choices in order to guide us and help us learn from our mistakes. Beware of getting in the way of those consequences. The story of the Prodigal Son says that when no one helped the Prodigal, *then* he "came to his senses" and sought his father. We ought always to point toward appropriate dependence on God, not chronic dependence on us.

THE BURDEN OF INTERCESSION

I've experienced the joy of introducing many to Jesus. But I am still waiting for the ones I love the most—many in my family—to join me in loving Jesus and knowing God personally. Some of us are deeply concerned about the realities of heaven and hell and our loved ones' lack of preparation for eternity. Some of our loved ones are involved in cults or false religions or have knowingly rejected the love of God. Faithfully stand in the gap between them and God, and bridge the gap with prayer. Represent your loved ones before the Father, and represent the Father to them. That gap can seem like a dark canyon, with only the echo of your prayers for company. It seems so foreboding, so wide, so lonely, so empty.

Sometimes we're not even aware of all the helpers the Lord has provided. Intercessors pray over regions where our loved ones live. People even pray for the names in phone books. Neighbors, doctors, and business acquaintances have surely prayed for our family members' salvation over the years. We cannot see all the help he has given, but I believe he sends helpers in prayer and in witness.

If the Lord has made you an intercessor for struggling family members or for those who have yet to accept Christ as Savior, remembering his promises will reassure you that you'll never really stand alone in that gap. When we intercede for our loved ones, Jesus intercedes with us, presenting our prayers to the Father. The Holy Spirit helps us to pray, angels cheer us on, and all of heaven awaits the answer and is encouraged by our perseverance. Jesus is our faithful prayer partner, our supportive brother, our available friend and constant helper.

Ask the Lord, also, for the blessing of divine assistance. I have asked for my loved ones to be given dreams, visions, the conviction of the Holy Spirit, whatever it takes for them to have ears to hear and eyes to see and hearts that will receive the forgiveness of Jesus. Jesus gave us beautiful images of heaven, but he also spoke of hell. Read about it, and tremble for the fate of those who refuse to follow Jesus. If we truly love our families, friends, and neighbors, we must persevere in prayer for their salvation.

UNDERSTAND RELATIONSHIP PRIORITIES

Don't allow grief over your siblings' or parents' decisions and actions to spoil the happiness of your own home. Your children deserve cheerful, energetic parents. Your spouse deserves an attentive and affectionate partner, not someone constantly depressed by family problems. If the pain is so great that you do become depressed, seek out a Christian counselor or a friend to help work through your sorrow over your loved ones rather than subject your spouse or friends to the constant weight of it.

The Word says to leave our fathers and mothers and cleave to our wives or husbands. If we are married, we are to separate and move our primary loyalty from our families to our chosen families. Our spouses and children come first. Sometimes we have to consciously prioritize our use of time and finances. At those times we must depend on the Lord's direction. Sometimes he will ask us to defy common sense and give when we don't have enough for our own needs, like the widow of Zarephath who "neglected" her son and herself to feed the visiting prophet (see 1 Kings 17). When God asks us to give to others, he provides enough for all.

EMBRACE THE HONOR OF INTERCESSION

Carrying others in prayer can grow tiring. But would you rather be your weaker brother or the one who bears the infirmities of the weak? Never envy the sick in spirit! It is so much better to be the strong one who tears up a roof to get a brother to Jesus than to be the helpless brother on a stretcher, completely dependent on others to get him to Jesus (see Mark 2). Yes, that person receives sympathy that you do not. That person receives attention that you do not. But do you want sympathy and attention, or do you want to enjoy the many blessings of spiritual health? I believe that being given the commission of faithful prayer and a consistent testimony is actually a glorious honor that will be well rewarded in God's eternal kingdom. To fight the way through the front lines while holding the hands of weaker brothers who struggle behind you is a place of spiritual honor. And as the Lord flows grace and strength through you to those in need, you also will benefit from the overflow.

WHY DOES GOD BURDEN YOU SO?

Perhaps your loved ones' problems are not a distraction from your journey but are really an integral part of your journey, an assignment from heaven for your growth and theirs.

Have you ever prayed to be like Jesus? Maybe you picture

Jesus surrounded by little children or feeding the thousands or being transfigured in glorious array. Do you remember that Jesus was so in agony that he sweat drops of blood in the Garden alone, abandoned by his friends even though he begged for their partnership in prayer? Do you remember that he was misunderstood, falsely accused, forsaken? Do you remember that he left a perfect home with a perfect Father to willingly carry the burdens of this horribly dysfunctional family of man? Love is often difficult, costly, and painful. The result of sacrificial love is delightful and joy filled. But the journey there can be arduous and taxing. The Resurrection that brought so much joy was the result of love. The Crucifixion that brought so much sorrow and grief was the act of love. We are to share, in a small way, in his sufferings. How else can we begin to appreciate God's great gift of redemptive love?

THE FRUIT OF A FAMILY BURDEN

Noah toiled for years to save his family from destruction. Joseph's faithful service to the king saved his undeserving family. Rahab's kindness and courage spared all her household. Esther risked her life to plead on behalf of her people. Ruth's commitment to family love redeemed them.

If God has burdened you to pray and intercede for your loved ones, you can be sure he will answer those prayers. He is not willing that any should perish. You know your prayers are in agreement with God's heart when you pray for another's salvation. Do your part. God will do his.

TURN A WISH INTO FAITH, HOPE, AND LOVE

Saying "I wish" about your family circumstances doesn't help. We can wish all we want, but then we have to return to reality. We have to accept the loved ones we have and love them the best we can. Every time you hear yourself sigh, "I wish," say instead, "In Jesus' name, I pray. . . ." Now things will change! In heaven we'll have our prayed-for loved ones safe beside us in the place where there are no more tears and no more pain.

LETTING GO

Letting go does not mean to stop caring—
　　it means I can't do it for someone else.
Letting go is not to cut myself off—
　　it's the realization I can't control another.
Letting go is not to enable—
　　but to allow learning from natural consequences.
Letting go is to admit powerlessness—
　　which means the outcome is not in my hands.
Letting go is not to try to change or blame another—
　　it's to make the most of myself.
Letting go is not to fix—but to be supportive—
　　it's not to judge but to allow another to be a human being.
Letting go is not to be in the middle arranging the outcome—
　　but to allow others to affect their own destinies.
Letting go is not to be protective—
　　it's to permit another to face reality.
Letting go is not to deny—
　　but to accept.
Letting go is not to nag, scold or argue—
　　but instead to search out my own short comings and correct them.
Letting go is not to criticize and regulate anybody—
　　but to try to become what I dream I can be.
Letting go is not to regret the past—
　　but to grow and live for the future.
Letting go is to fear less
　　and live more.

Author Unknown

Spread love everywhere you go: first of all in your own house.
Give love to your children, to your wife or husband,
to a next door neighbor. . . .

Let no one ever come to you without leaving better or happier.
Be the living expression of God's kindness; kindness in your
face, kindness in your eyes, kindness in your smile;
kindness in your warm greeting.
Mother Teresa, *In My Own Words*

I don't need to write to you about the Christian love that should be shown among God's people. For God himself has taught you to love one another. Indeed, your love is already strong toward all the Christians in all of Macedonia. Even so, dear brothers and sisters, we beg you to love them more and more.

1 THESSALONIANS 4:9–10, NLT

Dear Lord, among the ones I love, I ask you to heal wounds I've inflicted and wounds I've endured. Soothe and heal wounded relationships with the healing balm of your love. Heal the souls of the ones I love, and let them enter into the joy of your salvation. In the name of the Great Physician, amen.

nine

GOD'S AMBASSADOR OF LOVE

representing heaven to earth

Sometimes I get mixed up and imagine that I am generating love from my own sweet heart and that it's my love and my prayers that prompt and move the heart of God to action. That's not the way God's love works. Jesus did only what he saw the Father doing and what the Father asked him to do. He was God's ambassador of love on earth. Now, as the body of Christ, we are also commissioned as God's ambassadors of love.

AN AMBASSADOR'S JOB DESCRIPTION

God is love, and we are the ambassadors of his love. He orchestrates kingdom plans. We wait for orders and follow them. He makes great leaders out of humble, diligent followers of Jesus. Any messages of love we deliver originate from God's heart. We are privileged to share his burdens, his desires, and to pray and act toward the fulfillment of God's plans.

We represent heaven's interests on earth. We represent the people we care for in intercession before God's throne. Then we represent God to the people he loves by the way we live our lives and through the messages from heaven we deliver, whether they're spoken, written, performed, or given as gifts of service or sacrifice to the ones he loves. The job of ambassador is a great honor and joy. It's exciting and rewarding. Still, no matter how much we love our place of service and the people we serve, every true ambassador sometimes longs for home. We long for our homecoming, when Jesus will say, "Well done, good and faithful servant."

AMBASSADOR AND SERVANT

God made my role as ambassador and servant clear to me some time ago while I was praying for Michelle, one of my sister Sylvia's daughters. Sylvia sometimes calls her own daughter Linda because Michelle resembles me so much in appearance and personality. She laughs just like me and is a fun-loving young woman. I hardly ever get to spend time with her, though, since she is a busy student at the University of California, San Diego.

When our church was planning the yearly women's retreat to be held at a site near UC San Diego, I called Michelle. "Michelle, I'll be in town soon. Let's get together! We'd love to meet you for dinner on Friday night."

During dinner we invited her to join us for the first meeting of our retreat that evening. She readily agreed. I could barely contain my excitement. I had prayed for Michelle since she was born and hoped she would have an encounter with God at our meeting.

On our way to the meeting and during the worship time I prayed silently and fervently. "Jesus, you know how much I love Michelle. She's so precious. Thank you so much for putting her in my life. But she needs you to guide her. Please call on her tonight. Meet her here. Touch her life in an unforgettable, inescapable way!"

After I had spent much time silently pleading on my niece's behalf, the Holy Spirit abruptly interrupted my impassioned intercession.

Linda, I am not the ambassador of your love. You are the ambassador of my love.

This shocked me right out of my intercession and into a time of meditation, a place of silence, rest, and waiting, where God actually gets to do some of the talking in prayer. God reminded me of his many plans of love already at work in Michelle's life, through her parents and upbringing, her walk through life so far, her friends, everything, right up to preparing her to come to the meeting that night. All I did as the ambassador was to extend the invitation.

Our prayers of love begin in God's heart and always agree with his purpose to redeem, to deliver, to help and strengthen. This is his work on earth, and I am to be his ambassador, waiting to carry out instructions instead of trying to be the commander in chief! My frantic pleadings ceased. I decided to relax and enjoy my time with God and with my niece, daughters, and friends.

Though Michelle was unfamiliar with our style of worship, she lifted her hands to God and smiled as she sang. Later the speaker ministered to her personally and led her in a prayer of salvation and surrender while her three cousins and I wept with happiness.

Michelle had such a beautiful meeting with the Lord that night that she immediately went to a phone and called her boyfriend. "Nathan, I met Jesus! You've got to come and meet him here tomorrow night!"

Nathan must love Michelle very much because the next day he bravely accompanied her to the women's retreat. As our meeting began, I asked him to sit with us in the front row so that he could try to forget that he was the lone male in a room packed with women.

Nathan listened intently to the minister's every word. Through the speaker God seemed to address every question and need he had presented to God recently in prayer. The secrets of his heart were revealed in the most loving, kind way one could imagine. He came forward to publicly accept forgiveness and begin a new life.

Then the minister told Nathan and Michelle that they had an appointment with God on a Saturday night at Living Waters Fellowship in San Diego and that they should keep that appointment so that they could keep the joy they felt that night. The minister was from Kentucky and knew nothing of local churches, but after the service, Michelle and Nathan told me that fellow students were constantly inviting them to go to the Saturday evening services at Living Waters. God certainly does a thorough job with an invitation. His extravagant love had devised a plan that was much more complete than mine would have been. My sweet Michelle not only had an encounter with God, but God gave her a partner to walk with in Nathan and a place to walk to, to establish her steps.

After that special weekend I continued to love my niece, and Nathan, too. I prayed for them and sent them some old and new tools of discipleship, Bibles, and Christian music CDs.

God showed them his love in such a beautiful way. But I do feel I would have planned just one thing a bit differently. Nathan will have a few awkward moments in life. Whenever he gives his testimony of salvation, he will have to explain why he first met Jesus at a women's retreat!

AMBASSADORS DELIVER GIFTS FROM HEAVEN

If we volunteer as God's ambassadors of love, we may be on the job at times when we aren't even aware of the assignment. God simply puts us in the right place at the right time for divine appointments. Or he impresses ideas on us. We think we're just dancing through life, while God is actually choreographing our steps. God illustrated this beautifully for me one Sunday morning in our church.

During the Sunday worship service, while announcements are made, we also include a brief award presentation. I give a short speech describing what the honoree has done for the church or the community and then present a certificate, a "badge of honor," and an inexpensive gift. Someone also takes a photo and places it on a special bulletin board.

The appreciation gift is usually something inexpensive and silly, like a "champagne" bottle of pink bubble bath or a giant tube of Tootsie Rolls.

The first Sunday of the month is Family Worship Sunday, with a service geared to kids. This gives our Kids Church teaching staff a once-a-month break and allows the younger set to join their parents in worship. On that Sunday we choose the child who is to receive the award. I spend a little more, skip the gimmicky stuff, and buy a nice game or toy to give to the child. This particular time I conferred with our children's minister, and we chose two honorees: Frances, for her sweet helpfulness, and my daughter Alex, for being, at age thirteen, the youngest volunteer ever to be a Sunday school assistant at our church.

Ambassadors of love are on duty at all times.

Frances is a precious ten-year-old bundle of sweetness who makes homemade cards for folks when they're feeling down. She once wrote me a colorful crayoned card that read, "I love you. Everybody in church loves you!" underlined three times in purple crayon. Angels played harps for my ears alone when I read that card. Frances has a ready smile and a cheerful word no matter how tough her little life is, and it has been tough. She lives with her grandparents, both of whom suffered unemployment for a time.

I wanted to get a new dress for Frances but worried about church politics. The dress would cost more than we usually spend. I didn't want to provoke jealousy in others, but I was certain that the perfect gift for Frances would be a new dress. Pretty things are important to a girl her age. But if I got clothes for Frances, I'd have to do the same for Alex. That could raise questions about why we're presenting such nice gifts when the pastor's daughter just happens to be one of the recipients. Although I worried about the possible consequences, I felt certain of my leading from God about this gift, so I persevered in my appointed task, deciding that Jay and I would purchase Alex's award and use the church's gift budget for Frances's.

On Saturday my teenage shopping expert, Amanda, and I went shopping for Frances and Alex. We went to a large local department store and instantly spotted *the* dress: blue sunflowers on a pale blue background, a little bit fancy, and just Frances's style. It was stunningly perfect. The price tag wasn't. Reluctantly we headed to the sales rack but kept returning wistfully to the blue dress. Nothing else seemed appropriate. We finally relented and got not only the blue dress but also a pretty blue sunflower hair clip for her long gorgeous hair.

Alex was easy. A bright sunflower skirt, matching T-shirt, and yellow sunflower hair clip, perfect for Alex's sunny personality. Amanda and I went home pleased with our good taste.

When my husband saw the gifts, he forecasted impending doom: jealousy, envy, and charges that I was showing favoritism. Although I put on a brave face and said that we had done our best and I felt sure that Jesus was happy with what we had done, inwardly I was quaking.

Sunday morning I faked complete confidence. Our childrens minister presented Alex's award, bringing the sunny smile to her face that I had expected. Then I presented Frances with her "Cheerful Helper" certificate, a smiley-face badge of honor, and a hug and gave a speech about Frances and her gift of encouragement. When I handed her the gift bag, she reached in and pulled the dress out by the hanger for everyone to see. Oohs and aahs filled the silence. Everyone started clapping because Frances's face suddenly shone from within with an expression of amazed delight and wonder. She found her grandma's tear-filled face. Skipping back to her with dress in hand, Frances exclaimed, "God is so good to me!"

After church Frances and her grandma couldn't wait to find me. They also had gone shopping on Saturday morning. Frances needed a new dress for a family wedding the next week. Hours before Amanda and I went shopping, Frances had spied the dress she wanted right away—the one with the blue sunflowers. She loved it, and her grandma loved it, but the price was too high. Frances valiantly returned it to the rack and headed for the sale items. She settled for a dress on sale for one-fourth the price of the dress she dearly loved. She thanked her grandma and forgot about the pretty blue sunflower dress. But Jesus remembered.

When Frances pulled her heart's desire out of that bag, the overwhelming love of the Lord was revealed to her in a way no Sunday school story could convey. That fatherly gesture from heaven will forever remind Frances of how Jesus cares about her desires as well as her needs. Her grandma will always remember that God provides. Amanda will always be amazed at how God worked through her, even while she was just shopping with her mom. And everyone got a beautiful reminder of God's love because Frances and her grandma testified of God's goodness the next week and made everyone's heart glad.

Ambassador mission accomplished. God chose a gift for Frances, and I had the joy of delivering it. To be Christ's ambassador, we must seek to please God and not concern ourselves with trying to please everyone else. The fear of man can hinder us in our appointed rounds.

Afterward Jay said that if the only good thing we ever accomplished in our church was to buy that dress for Frances, it would be enough for him. He also said he would be more trustful of my "spiritual gift" of anointed shopping. The steps of the righteous are ordered of the Lord, even in shopping malls. Ambassadors of love are on duty at all times.

A woman missionary visited a remote jungle village to introduce the natives to Jesus. She told them of His kindness and His love for the poor, how He went to their homes to eat with them, how He visited them when they were sick, how He fed the hungry, healed the sick, bound up the wounds of the brokenhearted, and how children loved to follow Him.

The eyes of the natives lit up, their faces beamed, and one of them exclaimed: "Miss Sahib, we know him well; he has been living here for years!"

The story goes on to tell of the man they recognized, a missionary who had become a great ambassador of Jesus.

KEN GIRE, *Windows of the Soul*

All this newness of life is from God, who brought us back to himself through what Christ did. And God has given us the task of reconciling people to him. For God was in Christ, reconciling the world to himself, no longer counting people's sins against them. This is the wonderful message he has given us to tell others. We are Christ's ambassadors, and God is using us to speak to you. We urge you, as though Christ himself were here pleading with you, "Be reconciled to God!"

2 CORINTHIANS 5:18-20, NLT

Dear Lord and King, make me a faithful ambassador of your love. Let my countenance be like a postcard from heaven; let my words be like a message from heaven; and let my deeds be like a gift from heaven. Send me on my daily assignments, and give me good success. In Jesus' name, amen.

ten

GENEROUS LOVE

loving with all you have

We all came into this world owning nothing but a name. Since then, most of us have accumulated quite a bit we call our own. Lovers of God will look for opportunities to use their many possessions in service to the King.

Several years ago our family grew in the conviction that we should own only what we actually use from day to day and give the rest away as a blessing to others. In God's economy, everything should be put to use. As we made the transition from being avid consumers and collectors to a simpler lifestyle, we looked forward to having less to store, less to polish, less to dust. Traveling light helps us redeem the time, especially at spring-cleaning time. It's easier to get through the world with fewer possessions to weigh us down. As we combed through our closets and cupboards, we discovered they were filled with items we used infrequently. We decided that if we hadn't used something in more than two years, perhaps someone else could put it to better use. A room air conditioner we were just storing became a welcome gift to a Christian housing ministry. Unusual baking pans and kitchen tools went to a young lady who is constantly baking cakes for weddings and preparing fancy food for celebrations. We handed down clothes to friends and family. Other items went to charities to sell in their thrift stores to raise funds.

For a decade I had saved perfectly good but unneeded

furniture, dishes, and household goods for the time my children moved out and might need those items. Our garage was filled with items to furnish their future homes. A few years before our oldest was due to leave the nest, we encountered a newly divorced mom trying to establish a home with essentially nothing. I held a meeting with my older girls. "Remember all the things in the garage that we've been saving for when you move out? Well, you know Sally's predicament. Four kids and an apartment with nothing in it. It seems strange to me to know that four little kids have no place to sit and do their homework or eat dinner together, no dressers for their clothes, no beds, while we have all those things just sitting in our garage. What if we gave all those things to Sally's family? Then, when it's your turn to fill up a home, we can trust God together to provide for you the way he is going to provide for Sally. We could go yard-sale hunting and have lots of fun getting things when they're needed instead of just storing all this stuff. What do you think?" Fortunately the girls felt enthusiastic about helping our neighbors and experienced real happiness as we loaded up a borrowed truck to deliver the furniture and household goods. My girls felt well rewarded by Sally's tears and the beaming faces of the children as their empty apartment became a cozy home.

John, the apostle of love, writes: "If anyone has material possessions and sees his brother in need but has no pity on him, how can the love of God be in him? Dear children, let us not love with words or tongue but with actions and in truth" (1 John 3:17-18).

After Zacchaeus, the formerly avaricious tax collector, met the Lord, he gave the Lord his heart and his possessions: "Zacchaeus stood up and said to the Lord, 'Look, Lord! Here and now I give half of my possessions to the poor, and if I have cheated anybody out of anything, I will pay back four times the amount.' " (Luke 19:8). The allegiance of his heart had shifted from worldly wealth to heavenly values of mercy and justice. This was the pattern for the early church and for many who still choose to live in community as believers. "All the believers were one in heart and mind. No one claimed that any of his possessions was his own, but they shared everything they had" (Acts 4:32). We don't have to live in community to let go of our claim to our possessions and release them into the Lord's hands. Many of our things are performing perfect service right where they are in our own homes. But what do we have that is being wasted, rusting, or rotting from lack of use? Can the Lord use it elsewhere?

A MANAGER OF BLESSINGS

To grow in generosity, we need a fresh perspective on ownership. The Christian owns nothing. The follower of Christ is a steward, a manager of blessings lent by God, not an owner. All we have belongs to God. He made the earth and everything in it. It is God who enables us to create wealth (Deuteronomy 8:18). When we "give" something to God, we are like a daughter who proudly offers her mother a bouquet of daisies from her mother's garden or like a son who buys a gift for Daddy with the allowance Daddy gives him. All our offerings to God are merely portions of his extravagant gifts to us. But God is so pleased when his children take after him and learn to share.

Giving is a significant part of loving God and loving others. Giving to God goes beyond the basic tithe to an awareness that God should have control over 100 percent of our finances and possessions. The tithe is a modest beginning. A loving and joy-filled heart will look for every opportunity to do good through sharing this world's goods.

Those who look toward heaven hold lightly to this world. Elisabeth Elliot writes in *Love Has a Price Tag:* "For one who has made thanksgiving the habit of his life, the morning prayer will be, 'Lord, what will you give me today to offer back to you?'" This is the prayer of one who loves the Lord with all she has.

GIFTS SPEAK THE LANGUAGE OF LOVE

When I pray for people, they thank me. When I work alongside others, they thank me. When I express love and affection, people thank me. When I give someone my possessions or my money, there are thanks and tears and wonder, and the recipients never forget the gift. Why is that? My prayers are a gift, and my work is a gift, and my affection is a gift, but perhaps money speaks volumes about love because of the value this world places on it. People know that if we give them our "treasure," we have also given them our hearts. For Jesus said, "Where your treasure is, there your heart will be also" (Luke 12:34). When you share your possessions, you share a bit of your heart as well.

Our attitude toward giving is a barometer of spiritual health and coincides with other indicators of the fruit of the Spirit. Jay and I use a clergy tax consultant to help us with our taxes each year. He once told us, "There are two kinds of ministers who use our services. For some, ministry is a business. Their donation amounts are minimal, not even up to the standard 10 percent. But I know this when I meet them, for they are often marked by impatience or cynicism or a sour outlook on life. Others are in the ministry because they love Jesus. I can tell they are givers before going over their records. There is a joy, a peace, and an obvious love that emanates from them. Then we calculate their taxes, and the fruit of generosity is there. Sometimes you wonder how they can give so much on a salary of so little." The way we give reflects a life of love.

SHARE YOUR BEST

True lovers want to give their best, not their leftovers. On Paul Harvey's broadcast that aired on November 22, 1995, he shared this insight: "The Butterball Turkey Company set up a hot line to answer consumer questions about preparing holiday turkeys. One woman called to inquire about cooking a turkey that had been in her freezer for twenty-three years. The operator told her it might be safe if the freezer had been kept below zero degrees the entire time. But the operator warned the woman that, even if it were safe, the flavor had probably deteriorated, and she wouldn't recommend eating it. The caller replied, 'That's what we thought. We'll just give it to the church.'"

As every pastor and missionary knows, this story is all too true. Church fellowship halls are often furnished with the castoffs from our living rooms. The parsonage isn't always something most church members' families would want to live in. Let's turn that around and start providing our best for others. Think how special your church's missionary families would feel if they opened up a "care package" to find brand-new clothes in the right sizes for their children instead of mended castoffs. A truly loving giver makes do for herself and gives the best she can to others.

O ur attitude toward giving is a barometer of spiritual health and coincides with other indicators of the fruit of the Spirit.

One time I asked our local Christian bookstores for donations to give as door prizes at an upcoming conference for pastors' wives. I called the stores, explained the event, and asked if they'd like to donate something. Each store owner answered positively, so I looked forward to our appointments. At the first store the owner had forgotten our appointment, so she made her choice while I was there. She headed straight for the sale table, carefully examined each price tag, and finally decided on a very small basket of dusty artificial flowers. It had nothing to do with ministry and was the kind of thing I could pick up at a yard sale for fifty cents. Dumbfounded, I said thank you, went to my car with the paltry offering, and wept, wondering, *Is this all they think of us?* Miserly giving is nothing but a discouragement and is sometimes an insult. It doesn't do much for public relations either. Two other stores gave generous and meaningful gifts that overwhelmed the recipients. Our church shopped at those stores from then on.

Extravagant giving is always an encouragement. When someone gives their best, sometimes even sacrificing beyond their means, the gift brings a sense of awe at the goodness of God. Thankfulness and blessings flow both to the giver and to the receiver. Although many people don't realize that Jesus was the first to say, "It is more blessed to give than to receive" (Acts 20:35), they often repeat this maxim because almost everyone has experienced this truth. The joy of giving to honor others, to cheer them, to meet others' needs, or to make their lives easier is indeed a blessing we should give ourselves often.

What if you really don't have much to give? Ask the Lord

for more creativity in giving. Share what you do have. When you lose weight and happily shrink into new clothing in a smaller size, donate the larger clothes to a local charity. If you bake your own bread or cookies, make enough for neighbors. Go berry picking and pick up a gift that costs you nothing but time and a few scratches. Clean out your pantry, and pass on some of your surplus to a canned-food drive. I knew a teenager who gave more than twenty dollars a month to missions simply by denying herself. She carried a coffee can full of unspent change in her car. Every time she felt the urge to stop for a soda or ice cream or pick up dinner at a fast-food place, she took the money for it from her wallet and placed that money in her coffee can. Then she went home to eat more frugally. Besides supporting missions, she lost weight! Perhaps we could deny ourselves yet another shade of lipstick or another pair of shoes and find money we never thought we had for the Lord's work. Look around, pray, and think. The Holy Spirit loves to brainstorm with us!

ENOUGH IS ENOUGH

The Hanlon family lived in a lovely three-bedroom home that was just right for their four family members until Grandma moved in and another baby came along, all in one year. Suddenly, the only bathroom was always busy, the shared bedrooms brought on a barrage of sibling combat, and privacy was a thing of the past. The family began weekly prayer meetings for a new house. A bigger home would stretch the budget, but everyone was willing to eat beans more often and forgo a planned vacation to Walt Disney World so that they could live in peace and comfort once again.

They put their home on the market and began searching for a five-bedroom house in the same school district. In that neighborhood five-bedroom homes were rare, and Mrs. Hanlon never did find a home that matched the ambiance of their own custom-improved interiors. The more she looked at other homes, the better her own home looked. The kids started fussing about losing their neighborhood friends. And although it was a good sellers' market, no one made an offer. Not one. After six months

of frantic cleaning before every open house, they took their home
off the market and decided God had said no to their prayers.

The same day the house came off the market, a message
arrived from heaven in the form of a new issue of *Christianity Today*.
Sometimes God likes to say a little more than yes or no. This time
he wanted to teach a lesson in contentment. During the baby's nap
Mrs. Hanlon picked up the magazine and cried tears of repentance. That evening at the dinner table she read aloud portions of
the article "Trapped in the Cult of the Next Thing," in which the
author, Mark Buchanan, tells of his visit to a thatch-roofed
church in Uganda and a woman's testimony of God's goodness:

> "Oh," she said, "God is so good to me. I praise him all
> the time for how good he is to me. For three months, I
> prayed to the Lord for new shoes. And look!" And at that
> the woman cocked up her leg so that we could see one
> foot. One very ordinary shoe covered it. "He gave me
> shoes. Hallelujah, he is so good." And the Ugandans
> clapped and yelled and shouted back, "Hallelujah!"
>
> I didn't. I was devastated. I sat there hollowed out,
> hammered down. In all my life I had not once prayed for
> shoes. And in all my life I had not once thanked God for
> the many, many shoes I had.
>
> What I call enough is staggering lavishness to the rest of
> the world. A woman from a poor village in Bangladesh was
> visiting a Christian family in Toronto, and the morning
> after she arrived she looked out the kitchen window of the
> people's home. "Who lives in that house?" she asked the
> woman from Toronto.
>
> "Which house?"
>
> "That one, right there."
>
> "Oh, that. No one lives there. That's a 'house' for
> the car."
>
> The woman from Bangladesh was nonplussed. "A
> house for the car," she kept saying. "A house for the car."
>
> I picture that woman, looking out my kitchen window
> and seeing my garden shed, puzzled, saying again and

again, "A house for the shovels. A house for the lawn mower." (*Christianity Today*, September 6, 1999)

That article was the beginning of a joyful adventure for the Hanlons. That night they decided to reassign the extra money they would have spent for a larger home. They had originally made a decision to allocate one thousand dollars more per month for the mortgage payment on a larger house. If they were willing to spend that on themselves simply for a greater level of comfort, why not spend it on the truly needy, the truly poor, the kinds of folks who house a family their size in a one-room shack with no plumbing? Suddenly their "unanswered" prayer had an answer that would answer prayers for many others. Now, each month, they have the delightful task of deciding just where that thousand dollars will go. The first month they were able to support a woman from India through a year of Bible college. Her prayers were answered because someone learned that making do can be a wonderful alternative. Since then God has used the Hanlons to answer the prayers of many others. And no one in the Hanlon home complains about the one bathroom and the crowded conditions anymore. They are experiencing a new joy in giving and a new contentment with what they have. They've discovered the deep satisfaction of sharing in Jesus' concern for the poor.

WE ARE ALL RICH

How many times have we average folks complacently depended on "the rich" to meet the church budget or bankroll the mission project or give to nonprofit organizations? If you are looking to the rich, look in the mirror. We are all rich and increased with goods! It is amazing what a simple change of perspective can do to change our hearts, our desires, our motives, our way of living. If we in the Western world pay attention only to the media, the product catalogs, the advertisements, the storefronts, and the houses of our neighbors in the nicer part of town, we may end up with a skewed view of what is necessary for a happy life. In reality most of us live well above the world's average standard of living. In many countries the housing is poor, the diet is inadequate, supplies are sparse, and medical attention is insufficient at best. Get a copy of a *World Vision* magazine, or even *Time* or *Newsweek,* and you will discover that we in the Western world are wealthy. Absolutely wealthy. We have far more than most of the world's population whom God created and loves. We have far more than we really need. So why have so few of us learned a basic grace of childlike faith, the grace of giving and sharing?

WHAT ARE WE AFRAID OF?

Perhaps we are selfish. But I think more often we are simply afraid. Afraid for our futures, afraid we won't have enough, afraid we won't get to do what we want to do, afraid of being taken advantage of.

A wealthy friend with an empty nest recently made better use of his large home by opening it to a single mom with three young children and another young woman with no family. While he was on an executive retreat, someone asked him, "Aren't you afraid when you take in people you barely know? What if things turn up missing? A watch, some jewelry, all the valuable things you've collected from around the world? Aren't you worried?"

My friend replied, "I don't own anything that is more important to me than people. I would rather help people than worry about things."

Holding back because of fear indicates a lack of faith in God's provision. The Word of God is very clear about God's laws of supply and demand:

> Remember this—a farmer who plants only a few seeds will get a small crop. But the one who plants generously will get a generous crop. You must each make up your own mind as to how much you should give. Don't give reluctantly or in response to pressure. For God loves the person who gives cheerfully. And God will generously provide all you need. Then you will always have everything you need and plenty left over to share with others. As the Scriptures say, "Godly people give generously to the poor. Their good deeds will never be forgotten." For God is the one who gives seed to the farmer and then bread to eat. In

the same way, he will give you many opportunities to do good, and he will produce a great harvest of generosity in you. (2 Corinthians 9:6-10, NLT)

Old Testament theologian Walter Brueggemann writes concerning God's provision:

Three things happened to this bread, the manna, in Exodus 16. First, everybody had enough. But because Israel had learned to believe in scarcity in Egypt, people started to hoard the bread. When they tried to bank it, to invest it, it turned sour and rotted, because you cannot store up God's generosity. Finally, Moses said, "You know what we ought to do? We ought to have a Sabbath." Sabbath means that there's enough bread, that we don't have to hustle everyday of our lives. There's no record the Pharaoh ever took a day off. People who think their lives consist of struggling to get more and more can never sit down because they won't ever have enough." (*The Christian Century*, May 24, 1999)

A follower of God has the freedom to both work and rest. He has the freedom to use and share what God provides. There is no need to hoard God's provisions. They are continuous and reliable.

If we faithfully share what God gives us, he will continually replenish our supplies. God's laws ruling behavior are as sure as the natural laws he set in place. The law of gravity dictates that if you leap up, you will fall down. The law of giving says that if you give, God will give you more so that you can give again. Try it. Give something sacrificially, and watch God meet your needs. Give some more, and ask for more to give. Soon you will be addicted to the joy of giving. Ask God to remove all fear, all reluctance, all sense of "duty" and make you a cheerful giver and a generous soul. This will bless heaven and your world, but it will bless you most of all.

A GUARANTEED INVESTMENT

Ask anyone who was around in the 1920s and 1930s if there is anything resembling a guaranteed financial investment. A financial plan built on this world's best schemes, plans, and devices can collapse in a moment. Residents of God's kingdom hold many benefits, and one of them is a sure investment for their futures.

In the Gospel of Luke, Jesus speaks about the necessities of life:

> [God] will give you all you need from day to day if you make the Kingdom of God your primary concern. So don't be afraid, little flock. For it gives your Father great happiness to give you the Kingdom. Sell what you have and give to those in need. This will store up treasure for you in heaven! And the purses of heaven have no holes in them. Your treasure will be safe—no thief can steal it and no moth can destroy it. Wherever your treasure is, there your heart and thoughts will also be. (Luke 12:31-34, NLT)

I have now lived long enough that most of the furniture I have purchased new is worn out. Most of the clothes I have bought are worn out. The pleasures and entertainments I spent money on are long forgotten. In fact, most of what I have spent my money on is long gone and provides nothing for me now or in the future. Except for what I have given to God. All that I have given to God by sharing with his loved ones or giving directly to a church or other worthy work is stored up for me in heaven. My heavenly account keeps growing because of all the fruit my giving has nurtured. Everything I give with a cheerful heart is being used in the kingdom and will serve as a declaration of my love when the heavenly accounts are closed.

Everything we give back to God with a cheerful heart is used in the kingdom and will serve as a declaration of our love when the heavenly accounts are closed.

Do you still want to be rich? Then be truly and eternally rich—rich in good deeds and extravagant in giving. The apostle Paul instructs us:

> Tell those who are rich in this world not to be proud and not to trust in their money, which will soon be gone. But their trust should be in the living God, who richly gives us all we need for our enjoyment. Tell them to use their money to do good. They should be rich in good works and should give generously to those in need, always being ready to share with others whatever God has given them. By doing this they will be storing up their treasure as a good foundation for the future so that they may take hold of real life. (1 Timothy 6:17-19, NLT)

Many in the world today are living in homes built and funded by Christians, driving cars provided by or repaired for free by Christians, receiving free medical treatment adminis-tered by Christians, wearing clothes sent by Christians, playing with toys given by Christians, and eating food purchased and distributed by Christians. Through these works, the recipients see Christ's love for them. The love of God is found in Christ and is shed abroad in our hearts and then throughout the world. The people of the world can literally taste the love of God; they are literally warmed by the love of God; they are healed by the love of God. The love of God has come and met their needs. Through giving, followers of Jesus make God's love tangible, touchable, visible. Love the Lord with all you have, and help the world to see the love of Jesus Christ.

You can give without loving, but you cannot love without giving.
AMY CARMICHAEL, *The Book of Wisdom*

No one can serve two masters. For you will hate one and love the other, or be devoted to one and despise the other. You cannot serve both God and money.
MATTHEW 6:24, NLT

Dear Lord, all I have comes from you. I surrender all I have to you. Use it for your purposes. Cause me to excel in the grace of giving. Help me to minister your heart of love to the poor. Give me all I need to make me a blessing on this earth. In the name of Jesus, amen.

Eleven

DIFFICULT LOVE

loving someone you may not like

It was one of the dumbest prayers I've ever prayed, and God answered it right away. Ten years earlier God had called me into a public ministry to clergy families. At that time, having just emerged from a vicious attack waged by professing Christians, I bargained with God: "Yes, I'll do this—but only if you protect me. I'll welcome constructive criticism, but spare me from petty nit-picking. And nothing brutal! I just don't have the courage to stick my head up and be shot at again. I can't lead a ministry unless you save me from mean-spirited complaints and criticisms."

You might be thinking that this was the dumb prayer I mentioned, asking the impossible like that. Well, no, God honored that prayer. Not because he makes bargains with us, but because I think he knew I asked in sincerity for what I truly needed. It does seem to be a prayer in accordance with his will. Jesus does desire to see a lot less judging and criticizing in his church.

For more than a decade I directed Called Together Ministries. This was a behind-the-scenes ministry few people—except those in leadership circles—ever heard of, for that was our target audience. Still, I occasionally appeared on Christian television and radio and often in print. Even though I can be quite opinionated, I never received any letters or phone calls saying, "You are a theological doodlehead!" or "That's the most naive viewpoint I've ever read. Are you any relation to Pollyanna?" or the more polite, "I just want to say in Christian love that you are way off base and may not even be a real Christian since you don't agree with the way I think." No, nothing even remotely resembling that for ten years. Any public leader knows this verges on the miraculous.

On the ministry's ten-year anniversary I thanked God; then I prayed the dumb prayer I mentioned before: "God, I've grown in maturity, and I no longer require the pampering you've given me. I can take criticism now if you think I'd grow from it or be able to help someone else because of it. I've got my armor on, and I'm ready for arrows no matter where they come from."

THE ANSWER TO MY PRAYERS

The answer to my reckless prayer was swift in coming. I had written a poignant article on empathy for a denominational publication, and the publisher had thoughtfully included my ministry's address in the byline. One day I got a letter:

> Ms. Riley,
>
> Of course, we all know that you are a hypocrite. You say you love, but you do NOT!!!
>
> I am a widow and I have gone to many churches and have found NO LOVE!!!
>
> You are all a bunch of hypocrites. You don't really have any empathy at all and should not be writing about it!!!
>
> Harlots and whoremongers will enter heaven before you do!!!"

She signed off with her name and address.

My first thought was to file this in the round file next to my desk and forget about it.

Second, I thought about my recent prayer and meditated on God's faithfulness in swiftly responding to my every cry.

Finally, I remembered the part about how perhaps opening myself to criticism would help me or others. I couldn't find anything in the letter that might help me. But I did see a few clues that the writer wanted help.

Clue #1: Her letter had been written in very large letters with many exclamation points and much underlining. She was angry.

Clue #2: She mentioned widowhood and the church's lack of help. She was lonely, grieving, unhealed, and unhelped.

Clue #3: She signed her name. She wanted to be known. (Often angry letters are signed "anonymous.")

Clue #4: She gave her address. She wanted a response.

I prayed about what to do. Good intentions and feelings of sympathy toward someone are not enough. We must do what the Father wants us to do. Then I wrote back:

> I was very sad to hear that you are a widow and are now alone. That must be hard, and I am sorry for the hardship it has caused you. I am also sorry that churches and Christians have disappointed you. Please forgive us. Please look to Jesus who is the only one who ever lived who was perfect. He will never disappoint you. He loves you very much and would like to help you find some answers to make your life better.
>
> May I suggest that you contact some of the larger churches in your area and request information on a widows support group? Hospital chaplains and funeral home directors also usually maintain a directory of local support groups. Perhaps you will find some real empathy and answers.
>
> I'm enclosing a book on grief that many friends have found helpful. Also, please accept this gift as a token of my good wishes and prayers on your behalf. This teddy bear is from our family's personal collection of teddies. He is a good bear and has volunteered to leave our family and travel far away to keep you company. His name is

Alfred. My littlest one wants you to know it's always good to sleep with a teddy, even if you are a grownup.

May you know the love and peace of God.

Love,

Linda

I packaged "Alfred" up and sent him off, not having much hope. Perhaps she would spit on my cuddly offering, throw the book in the fireplace, and angrily denounce me again for such blatant hypocrisy.

But teddy bears can be a wonderful way to communicate love to others. Another letter arrived just a few days later. This time it was addressed to "Dear" Ms. Riley. The print was smaller, and the underlining and exclamation points were missing:

Dear Ms. Riley,

I was greatly surprised to receive your letter and your gifts. No one ever responds to my letters. No one has given me anything in a long time. As you know, there is not much Christian love in the world.

I will read the book. I have placed Alfred in my living room where the cat and I enjoy looking at him. Thank you for everything. I will try your suggestions.

This began a correspondence that was at times wearisome, for it was difficult to encourage my new friend. Apparently a root of bitterness had choked every flower from her garden. I could only send her little bouquets from my garden and hope they helped her look to Jesus as her source of love. Proverbs 18:19 says: "An offended brother is more unyielding than a fortified city." But Proverbs 15:1 says: "A gentle answer turns away wrath."

LOVE HAS THE WIT TO WIN

A dear old saint whom we called Elder Jim used to run the boys home at our church, a place where transient young men could stay awhile and get their bearings. Elder Jim, a retired school principal, was timid, but his gentle spirit and loving ways won every young man's heart.

One day my husband accompanied Elder Jim to one of his favorite places to minister, the streets of downtown Los Angeles. They decided to drop in at a bakery and have a snack.

The surly woman behind the counter glared at Jim impatiently. "Yeah, what do you want? I haven't got all day. Hurry up. There's other customers in the world besides you, ya know!"

Jay was about to teach the woman some lessons in etiquette when Jim, looking at her with moist, pleading eyes, quietly said, "It hurts my feelings when people speak to me like that." The startled woman stopped, lowered her head, then reached across the counter to pat Jim on the shoulder. "I'm sorry. Take your time. You just let me know when you're ready." She then waited on them, refilling their coffee and inquiring if everything was all right while other customers had to ask for refills. Jim's meekness and humility won a friend that day. He stopped in many times after that, and she was never gruff with him again.

My dad has often quoted a poem he learned at church: "They drew a circle that left me out. But love and I had the wit to win. We drew a larger circle that took them in" (author unknown).

When my niece Ruth was in the fourth grade, she endured months of torment from a bully who often excluded her from her group of playground friends. Loving auntie that I am, when I heard Ruth's lament, I silently thought that I would like to find the young tormentor and kick her in the shins. But Ruth had a better idea. She suggested inviting the girl to Knott's Berry Farm so they could get to know each other and become friends. Gathering my thoughts, I responded, "Oh yes, that's a good idea, right along the lines of what I was thinking." Ruth's kindness in the face of persecution is an example of love's strategy. The young lady became friendly to Ruth, although the truth is, that lasted only until after the excursion. Then she reverted to her mean ways. But Ruth still had the satisfying experience of rising above meanness and repaying good for evil. Had she repaid the girl in kind, her memories of the fourth grade would be much less pleasant.

LOOKING WITH ETERNITY'S PERSPECTIVE

To love the unlovely in our world, we must keep eternity in mind. Many visitors to our churches can seem quite unappealing on the surface, especially when we really obey Jesus' request to invite the poor, the homeless, and the disabled. Ask God to help you see people the way he does. Remember that when Jesus healed a blind man, the man required not just one touch from Jesus but two:

> When they arrived at Bethsaida, some people brought a blind man to Jesus, and they begged him to touch and heal the man. Jesus took the blind man by the hand and led him out of the village. Then, spitting on the man's eyes, he laid his hands on him and asked, "Can you see anything now?"
>
> The man looked around. "Yes," he said, "I see people, but I can't see them very clearly. They look like trees walking around."
>
> Then Jesus placed his hands over the man's eyes again. As the man stared intently, his sight was completely restored, and he could see everything clearly. (Mark 8:22-25, NLT)

So many times we need yet another touch from Jesus to see people clearly! When "undesirables" experience subtle rejection from church members, it becomes a stumbling block to their salvation or spiritual growth. Practice acceptance. Remember what is eternally important when it comes to dealing with the irritations of living and working beside others. It's easier to respond to offenses in a godly, exemplary way when we consider how our response affects our progress and theirs toward the kingdom of heaven. If we only considered eternity more often, heavenly hospitality and graciousness would take precedence over this world's ways. Keep a sense of eternity in your heart. The eternal viewpoint paints a different portrait of each of us, a portrait bathed in the light of love. Mother Teresa penned this verse:

Being happy with God now means:
Loving as he loves,
Helping as he helps,
Giving as he gives,
Serving as he serves,
Rescuing as he rescues,
Being with him twenty-four hours,
Touching him in his distressing disguise.

FROM *Teachings of the Christian Mystics*

I love the thought of looking for Jesus "in his distressing disguise." Jesus taught that whatever we do for others, we are really doing for him:

> "I was hungry, and you fed me. I was thirsty, and you gave me a drink. I was a stranger, and you invited me into your home. I was naked, and you gave me clothing. I was sick, and you cared for me. I was in prison, and you visited me."
>
> Then these righteous ones will reply, "Lord, when did we ever see you hungry and feed you? Or thirsty and give you something to drink? Or a stranger and show you hospitality? Or naked and give you clothing? When did we ever see you sick or in prison, and visit you?" And the King will tell them, "I assure you, when you did it to one of the least of these my brothers and sisters, you were doing it to me!" (Matthew 25:35-40, NLT)

The chapter goes on to illustrate that whenever we fail others, we are really failing Jesus. It is relatively easy to feel compassion toward a destitute and humble man or woman. But how about the poor in spirit? What about those who are surly, mean-spirited, antagonistic, pessimistic, those who have hardly any spirit left? It is a much greater task to love those people! We are blessing or hurting the heart of Jesus by the way we treat everyone. Therefore, treat everyone you encounter with dignity, respect, and outreaching love.

Floyd McClung Jr. writes in *Father Make Us One:* "The Scriptures teach that we cannot live the Christian life with integrity unless we love people when they are impossible to get along with. The Bible calls it unity. I call it 'doing love.' "

MY MISDIAGNOSIS OF GERTRUDE

We all know someone whose behavior leaves us perplexed and frustrated. And we'd all like to figure out how to eliminate difficult people from our lives—without hiring a hit man.

I'm speaking here of the type of person who sends me running to my old college psychology textbooks instead of to the Bible. After all, I need a diagnosis in order to know how to pray. Is this person BPD (borderline personality disorder), MPD (multiple personality disorder), or PHD (know-it-all personality disorder)? The fact that I am not a psychiatrist has never kept me from making a diagnosis.

I labeled Gertrude (of course it's a pseudonym—my apologies to anyone actually named Gertrude) as a "difficult person" because her behavior is chronically rude and terribly perplexing. After several hurtful, often public, incidents, my primitive instinct to avoid pain prompted me to keep a safe distance from fire, sharp objects, and Gertrude. I felt I needed to respond to her disorder in the healthiest way possible, so I went about following some fairly common guidelines for the kinds of situations I was encountering.

Each time she offended me, she repented. I said I forgave her. But I did not go further and accept her. I secretly considered her "incurable" and avoided her "like the plague." (Imagine comparing a person for whom Christ died to a disease!) I felt uncomfortable and truly wanted to do better but also felt absolutely incapable of a better response.

My husband, Jay, a truly Christlike man, repeatedly urged me to respond to this woman in a more loving, less self-protective way. But without real love for her in my heart, I really believed my attitudes and behavior could change only if her attitudes and

behavior toward me changed first. I knew Jay was disappointed in
me, and I felt the Lord's disappointment, too. But changing my
stance seemed almost impossible.

My solution involved "setting boundaries," which may
have been truly necessary in the beginning, but I patrolled the
boundary lines longer than I needed to, and the result was that we
were both "bound" from a real relationship. Although my solution seemed awkward, I continued relating to Gertrude according
to a prescribed formula.

Then the Lord showed me that formulas are fine for
infants—but wholly inadequate for mature Christians. The mature
partake of the Word. The mature imitate Christ. No wonder I felt
weak! I got my nose out of the textbooks and professional journals
and into the Bible. Through repentance, surrender in prayer, and
conformance with God's Word, I experienced a refreshing and
overwhelming refilling of love for the Lord, which then naturally
extended toward others. I was happy, Jesus was happy, and Jay was
really happy.

Formulas are fine for infants—but wholly inadequate
for mature Christians.

An important part of the answer for me was to pray
for humility. When I received this renewed spirit of humility,
my whole perspective changed. My friend's failings toward me
suddenly seemed like a speck of sawdust in comparison with
the redwood log of my failings toward her. After serious
prayer I called her—quickly, while still in my right mind—and
said, "I want to confess that I've treated you badly. I've judged
you. I've labeled you. After you repented, I would not allow
you to make a fresh start. I kept you at a distance. I said I
forgave you, but I didn't love you. I never let my defenses
down long enough to begin again. I robbed us both of a relationship that God meant to be edifying and helpful, even if it
was difficult. I hurt you by my cool politeness. I know you

couldn't help but feel the rejection when I held you at arm's length instead of embracing you. I'm so sorry. Will you forgive me?"

She was astonished. She cried. She thanked me. She then reviewed some of what had transpired between us in a revised version that would have irritated me before, but it didn't matter now. I felt completely accepting and was full of joy that she forgave me and that my apology had brought her happiness. I can't describe the feeling of exquisite freedom I experienced. Gertrude didn't have to change first. God changed me and started a "change reaction" that is still reverberating, affecting my friend, her family, and many others.

I thought I could really love everyone else if this troubled person would just get out of the way. Instead, it was I who needed to get out of the way and make room for more love, first in my heart, then in our relationship.

We've all encountered someone like Gertrude, perhaps a relative, a coworker, or a neighbor who makes life difficult. Jesus didn't stipulate that we should love our neighbors unless they're difficult and unpleasant. Since he commanded us to love our neighbors, all of our neighbors, we can be confident that his grace is sufficient to enable us to carry out his command of love. It's not that Jesus has the answer to everything. Jesus *is* the answer to everything. Making more room for Jesus means more room for peace, more room for love, more room for joy. His love compels us to eliminate the "difficult people" in our lives by recognizing who they really are, fellow strugglers whom Jesus loves, and loving them with the love of Christ. If they are worthy of God's love and patience, surely they are worthy of ours.

Do you have a difficult person in your life? Pray to see that person through the eyes of humility and love. Relationship does takes two. It takes Jesus and you. That is enough of a majority to turn things around in your relationships with "difficult people." Pray, bless, do good, and watch the thorn in your side become a bouquet in your hand.

Bitterness imprisons life; love releases it. Bitterness paralyzes life; love empowers it. Bitterness sickens life; love heals it. Bitterness blinds life; love anoints its eyes.

HARRY EMERSON FOSDICK, *Riverside Sermons*

Most important of all, continue to show deep love for each other, for love covers a multitude of sins.

1 PETER 4:8, NLT

Dear Lord, grant me understanding and compassion to continue to love those who don't seem to want my love. Let your fiery love burn away hardness, rejection, suspicion, and self-protection. Let there be nothing in my life that hinders love. In Jesus' name, amen.

twelve

LOVE IS KIND

serving through good deeds and kind acts

The language of love is kindness. This is how we communicate to others that they are valuable, worthy, treasured objects of our love and of God's love. Kindness sweetens our days and softens our memories.

Once, after I spoke to a woman's group on the joy of kindness, a woman approached me in tears, lamenting that she had lived an angry, resentful life that drove others away. Now, near the end of her days, bitterness and regret shrouded her memories. "I have wasted my life," she mourned.

I reassured her that it is never too late to learn to love: "Every morning, greet Jesus and ask, 'Give me an assignment of love today.' Perform at least one kind deed each day, not waiting for any gratitude or affection. Just be faithful to invest love in others, and later, the love you give will return to you." The kindness we show to others always returns to us, not necessarily from the object of our kindness, but often in other ways. God's precepts cannot fail. Proverbs 11:25 says: "The generous prosper and are satisfied; those who refresh others will themselves be refreshed" (NLT).

Kindness *is* refreshing. A friend who had done a generous deed shared this twist on a common saying from a thank-you note she received: "When life gives you lemons, make lemonade. But it is only the wisest and most generous of all who serve that lemonade to quench the thirst of others." Kindness is the sweetness that transforms something sour into something refreshing.

A few years ago I was diagnosed with cancer. My memories of the months I lived with cancer are sweet, partly because news of the cancer provoked an outpouring of love and kindness toward me. There were cards, phone calls, visits, untold amounts of prayer, help with chores, meals for our family. But these acts of love and kindness brought more than dinner or a clean house. They brought comfort and reassurance. Later God healed my cancer, so the frightening few months of uncertainty became a happy memory of a close walk with Jesus through a dark valley. The kind thoughtfulness of others made the way much brighter for my family and me.

FOLLOW THE LEADERS

There are so many ways to show kindness; the possibilities are endless. Think of your warmest memories. They probably involved the giving or receiving of kindness in some way. What has brought comfort and joy to your saddest days? Think way back. Perhaps a special teacher or your grandpa or a friend had a gift for kindness. Use these kindness memories as your model. Study the lives of those who make a habit of acts of kindness, and learn from their example.

GIVE THE GIFT OF YOURSELF

God has custom-designed each of us to do good works: "We are God's workmanship, created in Christ Jesus to do good works, which God prepared in advance for us to do" (Ephesians 2:10).

So many times we look at the visible gifts, the showy gifts, and wish we could sing, play an instrument, speak, or write. Then we could encourage others, we think! But public gifts are not the only options for a life of service. Some people are blessed with quiet and valuable gifts: a listening ear, a heart for hospitality, or patience with those who are slower in their walks with the Lord. You don't have to speak from a platform or write books to give gifts to someone else. Find your own place, and love people from there. Many are known for a "specialty" in the way they express kindness. We look forward to Sue's hand-decorated encouragement notes, Melissa's homemade berry jam, or Aunt Martha's offers of baby-sitting. What do you like to do? When you do it for others, it becomes an act of kindness.

DO EVERYTHING IN LOVE

God gives each of us particular talents and spiritual gifts that we can use to serve others. But he also produces in us the fruit of the Spirit, which grows and develops over the life of a follower of Christ. Galatians 5:22-23 lists this fruit as love, joy, peace, patience, kindness, goodness, faithfulness, gentleness, and self-control. Notice that love is listed first, and not by coincidence. Love is the most important, and it makes all the others possible.

Kindness sweetens our days and softens our memories.

Finding our particular niche of service can be difficult. But finding the starting place is easy. Galatians 5:13 instructs us how to serve: "Serve one another in love." The starting point of service is a heart of love for God and for God's people. When we serve out of a lesser motive, we build monuments to God made of wood, hay, and stubble. Many will be surprised to see their abundant works burned to ashes on Judgment Day when God tests them (see I Corinthians 3:9-15). Love, humility, self-sacrifice, the desire to glorify God—these are the enduring gold, silver, and precious stones of works that please the Lord. Every work, great or small, performed with love as the motivation, will withstand the fire of testing. Great works that drew much attention from the church will burn as stubble if they were not done in love. This is one reason why Jesus asked us not to judge before the time when the secrets of everyone's hearts shall be revealed. Only God can judge our hearts, and that is the key to judging our works.

PRAYER IS A KINDNESS

The kindest act we can do for others is to pray for them. When we do, we lift them up to the throne room, where the one who loves them most can meet their deepest need. An advantage to praying for others is that prayer causes us to see them in a more positive light. Praying for those you naturally love is a joy; praying for those you don't naturally love is a necessity. Prayer develops a sensitive heart in the one who prays. And sensitive words flow out of a sensitive heart. Your words will be more loving, kind, and patient because you pray. And don't forget to pray with friends whenever they share a troubled spirit or express a need. Do it right away, as soon as you hear of the need, or you might forget. Many serious intercessors keep a prayer journal with them to record needs as they arise, then record the answers to encourage them as they review them later. Thank God when the answer arrives. Keep a prayer list of those you love, and keep adding new acquaintances. Pray regularly for each of them.

LISTEN FOR INSTRUCTIONS

As you pray, the Lord may prompt you to reach out in various ways. Keep a notebook and pen handy to jot down ideas as the Lord brings them to mind. Two women in our church had a wonderful ministry consisting of simple gifts of encouragement that they offered with great love and joy. Each Sunday they looked around the church and chose someone to encourage: They prepared dinner and cleaned the home of a busy working mom. They gathered up a few dozen children and used the church nursery to provide child care for a "parents night out." They gave money to a single dad at Christmastime and baby-sat while he shopped. They befriended a newcomer and took her out for lunch and a walk on the local beaches on a Saturday. They wrote encouraging, affirming notes to people in church. Their acts of caring and kindness blessed the whole church.

Opportunities to practice kindness are abundant. Are you going to visit a friend with children? Grab some lollipops or home-baked cookies for the kids. Is someone in front of you at the grocery store short of change? Chip in, smile, and tell her to pass the favor on sometime. Is there a disagreement about what movie to attend? Let your friend choose. Practice loving-kindness until it becomes second nature. When you give love as a gift, it usually gets returned.

LOVING IDEAS

Some people seem to have no trouble thinking of ways to show kindness. Others find it more difficult. We can all stand to expand our list of ideas. Here are some suggestions. Try one idea each week, and watch your heart for others grow!

- Don't underestimate the simple act of smiling.
- Develop a prayer list of your family, friends, neighbors, and coworkers. Let them know they are in your prayers.
- Be friendly, polite, and liberal with *please, thank you,* and sincere words of affirmation.
- Really listen. Look people in the eye, and give them your full attention.
- Refrain from judging. Give others the benefit of the doubt. Help others live up to your good expectations of them.
- Learn local manners and observe them. A breach of etiquette is often judged as an unloving act even though it may have resulted from mere ignorance.
- Learn to say, "I'm sorry," with sincerity and humility.
- Share your time and that of your family graciously. If time boundaries are needed for your own family life, pray, discuss, and implement needed guidelines.
- Treat every call as if it is the most important one of the day. Let both your tone and your words say, "Welcome," not "Keep Out." Be kind even to telemarketers. They're just trying to eke out a living like the rest of us. Many are single moms or men who have suffered unemployment for some time. Decline with graciousness: "I'm sorry, but I'm not interested at this time. Thanks for calling."
- Say out loud: "I care about you." "I'll miss you when you're away." "I love you." "I'm so sorry you're hurting."
- If hugs, kisses, and "I love you's" don't come easily to you, practice! It feels great to be free to express love and affection.
- When someone expresses a need, do something about it. Provide

practical help, refer someone to a specialist, or when needs are chronic, refer to a professional to resolve the long-term difficulties.

- Volunteer for a service organization. Tape audio books for the blind, donate blood, work in hospice care, sort donations at the Salvation Army. Every service-oriented organization is looking for willing volunteers. Find your place, and enjoy it.
- Take a home-cooked dinner to shut-ins, new moms, and others under exceptional stress.
- Be prompt with get-well cards and expressions of sympathy. When people are in intense pain or grief, be with them as soon as possible.
- The first anniversary of a death can be difficult. Note the anniversary on your calendar, and time a card to arrive that day. Add a note remembering the loved one and offering prayer and solace to those still grieving. If you live nearby, ask how they would like to spend the day. Perhaps you can help by being there to listen and keep them company.
- Share what you already have: home-baked bread, garden produce, outgrown clothing and toys, extra furniture.
- Empty your storage areas. If you haven't used something in the last few years, chances are you won't miss it, and someone else may be able to use it. Give it away, or donate it to an organization.
- Teach a skill to a younger person. Make a friend for life by discipling that person in the Word or teaching a special skill such as sewing, wallpapering, canning, freezing, baking, fishing, waterskiing—whatever is fun to share.
- Clip coupons and share them—baby food and diaper coupons for young moms, favorite brands for your friends.
- Remember birthdays and anniversaries with a card.
- If you have the time and the stamina, offer to baby-sit occasionally for single moms or just plain hassled and harried moms.
- Remember the children. Carry a box of Tootsie Roll Pops, M&M's, or another candy that doesn't melt with you in your car for whenever you're visiting a home with children present. You'll become their favorite grown-up!

- Send thank-you notes promptly after receiving a gift or special help.
- Find something you can do to minister to those in need, either through financial contributions or volunteer service with an agency offering practical help to the poor. Jesus loves the poor. Volunteer to help feed the hungry on special occasions such as Thanksgiving or Christmas Day.
- Love generously. Pay your tithes and offerings to the storehouse of your local church, and support other worthy organizations as well.
- Give gifts of appreciation to pastors, teachers, and others who minister to you or your family. Small gifts provide big encouragement to those who are laboring in the harvest fields.
- Share what you have and sometimes even when you don't have it. Money speaks eloquently in the language of love. The Lord will repay your kindness and give you even more to share. God loves a cheerful giver!

The ideas listed above are just a few to get you started. There is really no end to the ways you can give the gift of kindness. If you struggle to come up with ideas on your own, how about getting together with a friend to brainstorm about creative ways to show kindness to others? Make it a joint effort. It's not important whether they are your ideas or someone else's. What's important is the encouragement others will receive as you put them into practice.

> One day a troubled heart told me of a thought which perhaps some of you have: "How can I love many people? I can love some very much but there is not room in my heart for many." I spoke to her of the bees and of how cell after cell is added to the comb and each is filled with sweet honey. Each cell is shaped that the greatest possible number can be fitted into the smallest possible space. God, who taught the bees to do this, can do something as wonderful for us. He can add a new cell to our heart as each new person comes to be loved. And He can fill each cell full of the sweet honey of His love.
>
> AMY CARMICHAEL, *The Edges of His Ways*

I myself have gained much joy and comfort from your love, my brother, because your kindness has so often refreshed the hearts of God's people.
PHILEMON 1:7, NLT

Dear Lord, help me to excel in kindness. Grant me creativity and spontaneity in the offering of good works and kind deeds. Refresh, encourage, provide, equip, comfort, and cheer through me. In Jesus' name, amen.

Thirteen

LOVE LETTERS

letting a letter speak love's language

Many have described the Bible as a love letter from God, the most powerful and moving love letter ever recorded. The written word is powerful. Our spoken words may linger for a time, but our written words live on and on. Putting love in writing gives it permanence.

Long ago I read a true story about a woman who became estranged from her father after an angry and painful exchange. Many months later her father suffered a heart attack and was admitted to the hospital. He asked that his daughter be notified. She rushed to the hospital but did not arrive in time to make amends and hold her daddy's hand on his way out of this world. Devastated, she turned to go home and grieve. Then a nurse handed her a small slip of paper. When the woman's father knew he would probably die before his daughter arrived, he left this note: "I'm sorry. Forgive me. It was my fault. I love you very much, and I'm proud of you, honey. Your dad."

That story moved me. It made me want to make sure that everyone I love is always positive of my love for them. What if there were some unpleasant episode before I died? What if I were driving to my sister's home and died in a car accident and she felt unreasonably guilty about that? It would be a wonderful gift to be able to preempt any unnecessary guilt or remorse a family member might feel. Now, because of the impact this story had on me, I've written love letters to a few dear friends and all my family members for distribution after I've died. The letters reminisce about our times together and how their lives enriched mine. I included affirmations of their admirable qualities and gratitude for things they've done for me. I made it very clear how much I love them and look forward to seeing them again in heaven. Even though I write love notes now to these same people, I want them to have this one last hug from me, one last kiss, one last "I love you" via a letter. This way I can be as extravagant with my affection as I please without fear of embarrassing us both. To those who have yet to meet Jesus, I can make a final and powerful plea to prepare to join me in heaven. I reassure them that I've asked Jesus ahead of time to let me go with the angels to meet my favorite folks when they make their transition to heaven. And if any go before me, I hope they will be part of my heavenly welcoming committee. Letters like these can provide a unique source of comfort at a time when the reader desperately needs such comfort.

Wouldn't you love to have a letter to read and reread from someone you can't talk to anymore? Why not do that for your children, grandchildren, sisters and brothers, special friends, and others who have been important to you? Make a last will and testament to the love you shared. Put the letters in a safe deposit box and rejoice that even after your death new blessings of love will flow from these last letters.

A LETTER ADDS WEIGHT TO OUR FEELINGS

The power of pen and paper adds weight to our words, for good or evil. Angry sentiments don't belong on paper, where the words live on long after the anger has died. Unfortunately for others I have learned this the hard way. But there is nothing like the power of the written word to convey love, affection, affirmation, and encouragement. A letter is a lasting reminder of your affection and warm wishes. A reader can refer to a letter again and again and receive ongoing encouragement. When you give the gift of a letter, it's as if you're setting your words in bold copy: I love you!

It's a thrill to receive a love letter from a spouse when he is on a business trip. You know he took the time to think about you.

He cared enough to make you feel loved and missed. It's a joy to open a love note with crayoned drawings from a young child. It's a comfort to get a card or note from old friends or new acquaintances saying, "I'm thinking of you." A file or box of love notes and thank-you letters can warm you from within when life's cold winds blow.

Putting love in writing gives it permanence.

A LETTER CAN DELIVER THE GIFT OF ENCOURAGEMENT

When I directed Called Together Ministries, I wallpapered my office with thank-you letters that arrived in response to our ministry. When I plastered my walls with these missives of gratitude, I knew that people might misunderstand and think that I had chosen wallpaper with the theme "How Great I Art." But I truly needed that wallpaper. I leaned on those walls when I grew tired. I often went to the office to work after getting all the kids to bed. While working long hours late at night, I often grew "weary in well-doing" and needed those reminders that all that work was worth it for the joy of providing inspiration, encouragement, and comfort to those in great need of it. Kind letters lent me strength for the work.

So many times we think that our work goes unnoticed and our efforts remain unappreciated. I have a friend who is tremendously blessed with a gift of helps. She excels at the details, the behind-the-scenes effort, while the people she assists earn many awards and receive copious amounts of affirmation. Although she gives her service to the Lord and does it for him, she still struggles with feelings of insignificance at times. One day a letter arrived addressed to her, not to the leaders of the ministry she assisted. The letter read:

> At the conference I recently attended, I noticed your hard work at the registration table and how you handled an

irritable lady with such graciousness. You helped her back into a better mood. I noticed how you saw to the details—seating arrangements, water for the speakers—your patience with all the small challenges. You are doing an important work and doing it with cheerfulness. The conference was a great help to me and my husband. The speakers were great. But could they do it without people like you? I noticed your hard work, and Jesus notices it every day. Thank you.

My friend framed the letter and humbly hung it inside her closet so she can be encouraged each morning as she dresses for work.

A letter of affirmation can make a great difference in the life of your pastor, coworkers, teachers, neighbors, business-people, just about anyone you meet. Let the boss know how kind and helpful an employee was. I once wrote a letter of affirmation addressed to supervisory staff, affirming the social worker who handled our first adoption. The staff pulled out that letter and others like it and read them aloud at her retirement party. She was glowing! And all the workers there shared in the blessing of affirming their important role in children's lives.

An employee at a local Borders bookstore shared her delight at receiving this letter:

I want you all to know I think you're great. My niece treats your bookstore like a library, and you generously allow that. My niece is only twelve, and her life at home is no fairy tale, thanks to stuff grown-ups do. The fact that she can escape the stress in her life for hours and feel welcome and safe in the warm and wonderful world of books is such a comfort to me. You shelter angels. Thanks for thinking more about people than about the sale condition of your inventory.

Is there someone you need to thank? Someone who needs to open her mailbox, read your letter, and feel her spirits lift?

A LETTER CAN BEGIN THE PROCESS OF HEALING AND RESOLUTION

Letters can heal hurts. A letter to a parent in which you remember positive aspects of your upbringing, special times together, a memorable vacation, or a life lesson the parent imparted can cheer up an aging parent who could use a reminder of his or her worth. A letter to an old and forgotten friend can revive a lost but valuable friendship. A note placed on the pillow of a teenager in the midst of the painful process of separating from her parents can build bridges: "Honey, you know I'm not too fond of that new tongue jewelry, but I sure am fond of you. You've always been unique, and I feel confident you will fill a unique and important place in this world. Love, Mom."

A letter can build a bridge over chasms of neglect.

A letter can build a bridge over chasms of neglect. Friendships and even family relationships can suffer from neglect when we let the hurry of life overtake us. A letter can open the door to a renewal of love: "I haven't seen you in so long. I confess I've allowed my life to become too busy for the truly important things of life, like my friendship with you. Would you forgive me? I'm going to be in your city next month and would love to see you. I'll call this week and see if we can get together and catch up."

A letter can also pave the way back to friendship when angry words have made the path rocky and treacherous. Begin a reconciliation with a letter. Of course, a letter inviting renewed relationship is only an invitation. A card or letter is only a one-way communication. We must love the other person enough to then engage in two-way communication and listen and under-stand the other's viewpoint. An apology card is an invitation to the face-to-face work of rebuilding love and trust. Is there someone in your life who needs you to open the door to future reconciliation?

EVEN ORDINARY LETTERS CAN BE SPICED WITH LOVE

Since my husband is a pastor, students often ask us to write letters of recommendation for college, job, and program applications. Recommendation letters can be boring, especially for those who must read dozens or hundreds of them. For their sake, I try to spice them up. The following is a portion of a letter I wrote for a young friend, Liberty Rudell, who was applying to Pepperdine University:

> We met Liberty when she was born on leap-year day of the bicentennial year, 1976. She was born in a special year on a special day, and she is a spectacularly special addition to the universe.
>
> Was it Walt Whitman who wrote, "The child is father to the man"? Well, it was somebody famous. Because the verse is true, we want to share a little bit about Liberty the child. Absolutely the most adorable, charming, bright-eyed beam of starlight that ever hit the earth. A joy to befriend, from the first time her tiny hand reached out to ours, until now, when her shadow looms taller than ours.
>
> As I write about Liberty, I can picture so many delightful times enjoying her bright company. She was raised with consistent discipline, overflowing love, and a lot of fun sprinkled on top. Her parents are what you would order out of a catalog, if one could order up a custom set of parents. Spiritual, intelligent, interesting, creative, generous, fun-loving, kind, friendly. They have passed all this on to their children. Their home is the place all the kids hang out because it is the warmest place around. An interesting thing about the Rudells is that they naturally attract and win others to Jesus. People want to have the relationship with God that they embody.
>
> If you are blessed to have Liberty on campus, the light level will suddenly increase. Other students who are going through darker times will be helped by Liberty. Her informal counseling skills, natural helpfulness, and relational abilities would be a valuable asset to any student body.

Liberty is creative, innovative, well organized, hardworking, goal-oriented, socially adept, outgoing, sensitive, and aware. She's the kind of person who will achieve her goals in life, the more challenging, the better.

I have tried to be balanced and think if there is anything in Liberty's personality, experience, or qualifications that would present a challenge to her success in college. But, honestly, I couldn't come up with anything but positives about her. She stands out as a flamingo among pelicans; a gazelle among porcupines; a human among amoebas. I could go on, but I'm sure you wish I wouldn't!

I hope this commendation isn't too glowing. That's what happens when you're around Liberty. You get a little stardust in your eyes. We love her very much. You will too.

And, yes, she was accepted and has graduated from Pepperdine. When I asked Liberty, now a career woman in her mid-twenties, if she had a copy of the letter I could use for this book, it took her exactly one minute to retrieve it. It's a prized possession. That letter will remind her of my love for her long after I'm gone.

LOVING LETTERS CAN GIVE COMFORT

Letters that offer condolences after a loss carry supreme importance, and people save and reread them again and again. While still a teenager, I had a friend who was arrested for being under the influence of drugs and alcohol. Tragically, while he was in jail, still not in his right mind, he hung himself. When I went to inquire at the police station, the police asked me if I knew anything about his next of kin. I had only known the young man for a few weeks while he came to our church, so I knew little about him. I went to his apartment and found his unlocked car outside. Inside the car I found a Mother's Day card already addressed to his mother in Murfreesboro, Tennessee. I took the information to the police, then sat down to write to his mother, including the card he had chosen and prepared weeks before Mother's Day. I told her about what a well-liked young man he was, about the efforts he had made to stop taking drugs, and about how much everyone at church loved him. I also told her how he was often homesick for his mom and family and said that he just wanted to get out of California, go home to Tennessee, and have a farm someday.

I thought the police had notified his mother by phone, but it turned out that the arrival of my letter brought the very first news of her son's death. We never know how important a letter can be. Perhaps it was better to learn of his death through a tender remembrance than through a police notification. I'm sure the Lord arranged it this way. We wrote back and forth for some time. Her own faith comforted her. She shared my first letter with several local pastors, who read it to their youth groups to illustrate the importance of staying away from drugs. She has kept my letters, and I have kept hers for nearly thirty years now. I still weep for her and her son when I read through boxes of sad and happy memories.

More recently a good friend died in a car accident. I knew that in the year before her death she and her husband had been making difficult decisions and had to work through some disagreements over how to resolve them. In my letter to her husband after my friend died, I relayed an entire conversation we had shortly before her death. She had commended her husband's good judgment and leadership abilities. Although they disagreed, she trusted him and cheerfully submitted to his leadership, not just in front of him, but in private as well. She had expressed many positive things about him, which I shared in the letter. The letter arrived just as he was wondering about those very things. It was exactly what he needed to know, and it put his heart at rest.

A condolence letter honors the love that lived between the one who passed on and the one you are writing to. It's a place to recall stories of life and love and to offer the bereaved your love, prayers, and practical help. You possess a unique perspective on the deceased person's life and contributions. And your letter will make a unique contribution toward healing their loved one's grief. We should accompany all of the letters we write with prayer, but we should particularly pray for inspiration before writing condolence letters. Share some of your memories of the person, whether they are poignant, humorous, inspiring, or just characteristic of the one who is gone. No one else can say it the way you can.

A LETTER IS ALWAYS WELCOME, WHETHER ELOQUENT OR SIMPLE

If you don't count yourself among the eloquent and writing is difficult for you, find a poem, an essay, a card, or even a comic from the Sunday paper that expresses your feelings, and send it with a brief note. Even simple words such as "Your life has made mine richer. I love you" make anything written with love a treasure to keep.

My father-in-law once read me a letter that his grandfather had written decades ago and sent to him when he was a young boy. In it the grandfather shared his everyday life, even recounting the antics of a squirrel he observed through the window near his desk. The letter didn't really have a point. The message seemed to be "I love you, and I think about you, and I'd like to share a little of my life with you." Reading it aloud in his sixties, my father-in-law still beamed with an expression one would find on an excited little boy just opening a letter from Grandpa.

Once, a woman at church confided to my husband that she wanted to write a thank-you letter for something I had done, but she felt intimidated by the fact that I was a writer. Jay reassured her that I would appreciate her note, so she went ahead. Her letter was simple and beautiful. Her thank-you note warmed my heart and went into the file of thank-yous I treasure.

Find some stationery right now, and write someone a letter filled with love and goodwill. Write it in your own special style. God will enlarge it in the heart of the recipient. Let a letter share your love.

> Eloquence is the power to translate a truth into language perfectly intelligible to the person to whom you speak.
> RALPH WALDO EMERSON, *Letters and Social Aims*

Dear brothers and sisters, we always thank God for you, as is right, for we are thankful that your faith is flourishing and you are all growing in love for each other.
2 THESSALONIANS 1:3, NLT

Dear Lord, inspire me with words of love. Inspire me to write letters that strengthen the weary, lift up the discouraged, bring joy, and express love. Bless people through my written thoughts. Give me words that will not only delight the reader but will delight your heart as well. In the name of Jesus, amen.

fourteen

POWERFUL LOVE

overcoming fear with love

I hate hospitals. I hate the smells, the grim faces of the waiting, the pained, weary faces of the recovering, the factory-like processing of anguish and distress. It's a rare Christian who ministers often inside hospitals. Sometimes I wonder, if more of us went to bring the love and power of Jesus into these dark places while we're healthy, perhaps fewer of us would end up in hospitals as patients.

Recently a pastor friend jokingly informed me, "I don't do hospitals." He does lunch. He does meetings. He does weddings, baptisms, and even funerals. But he somehow feels exempt from helping and encouraging people when they happen to be inside a hospital. Perhaps he was traumatized when he had his tonsils out at five and the clown visiting the children's ward gave him nightmares. Perhaps his aunt gave up the ghost right in front of him during his first-ever hospital visit. Who knows? All I know is that hospitals are full of hurting, questioning people and we might have to go in there to comfort them.

Years ago an accident transformed me into a regular hospital visitor. It wasn't my accident that took me to the hospital. It was Yolanda's. Yolanda was an imperfect stranger who went screeching by on a main thoroughfare. I commented to my daughter, "There's an accident waiting to happen." It didn't wait long. Two blocks ahead Yolanda met four cars full of strangers. Her van flipped over and came to rest upright, and Yolanda stumbled out just as I pulled alongside.

A large crowd gathered, but whether out of fear or repulsion, no one approached the injured. I locked my young daughter in the car and raced toward the most seriously injured, who happened to be Yolanda. Someone handed me a clean cloth from a nearby bar. I helped the staggering woman to lie down, cradling her head in my arms so she wouldn't be lying in the glass. She had nearly been scalped when her head hit the windshield. I applied pressure to her head wound to stop the bleeding while covering her eyes with the same cloth so she wouldn't see what was left of her shredded arm. Certain that her soul would soon enter eternity, I tried to ignore the crowd and help her soul as well as her body. I asked her name and had her pray after me. I helped her ask Jesus to forgive her sins and help her right now. She responded with an eagerness born of her recognition of her desperate state.

While I prayed out loud for her life, I also prayed silently that I would not lose my lunch on the poor woman because her appearance was so terrible. Her arm seemed beyond saving, her head was in horrific condition, and all she could say after praying was, "Oh, my stomach, my stomach, it hurts so bad." Then I looked down and noticed she was pregnant and seemed to be delivering at that moment.

After what felt like an eternity the emergency team arrived, and I was thankful to leave Yolanda's care to people who knew what they were doing. I gave an accident report to the police, picked up my other daughter from school, and went home to wash Yolanda's blood out of my hair and clothing.

Then I braced myself for the hardest part of the day—a visit to our local county hospital. This hospital is known for two things: the most excellent trauma care available and the worst hospital ambiance anywhere. The walls are painted a lovely shade of "Nausea Green"; the smell in the air is "Eau d'Antiseptic Masking Death and Decay." The staff are like robotons, when you can find any staff. The rooms and halls are crammed with people who all seem to be waiting for some assistance.

I went to the hospital and learned that the trauma had indeed induced labor. She had delivered a baby boy, three months premature and not expected to live. The doctors were trying to hold off on amputating Yolanda's arm. After three days, when Yolanda had improved enough to receive visitors, I entered her room with a gift for the baby, a tape player, and some Christian music tapes. When I introduced myself she cried out, "Oh, it's the voice of the angel who prayed for me! I thought it was a real angel!" After apologizing for not being an actual angel, I got to know Yolanda and discovered that she had been speeding away from God all her life. During subsequent visits I met many of her relatives who were believers. They felt that God had placed me not only at that street intersection but also at an intersection in Yolanda's life. For them, my being there to pray for Yolanda was just like having a trauma unit from God show up immediately on the scene.

I visited and prayed with Yolanda for several weeks. She recovered and was able to keep her arm, although not the use of it because of the extensive nerve damage. Her forehead is scarred with one long line of stitching, but she is still beautiful. Her son is a living miracle, with no impairment whatsoever.

Afterward many of my friends questioned me: Wasn't I afraid of a lawsuit for handling an injured person? Since the scene was so bloody, wasn't I afraid of contracting HIV? And how did I find the courage to pray out loud in front of a huge crowd of onlookers? Yes, I had been afraid. But love casts fear aside and gets on with the task at hand. What are a few moments of embarrassment compared with the eternal fate of a precious soul? Christ's love compelled me. I hadn't needed to reason with myself, "If my sister were dying on the street, wouldn't I want someone to hold her and pray for her?" If we walk in love, a loving response to crisis will be spontaneous.

Gradually I lost touch with Yolanda. But years later a beautiful young lady with a scar on her forehead walked into our church holding her young son's hand. It was Yolanda, and she wanted me to know that she and her son were serving the Lord.

I still hate hospitals. To move from a comfy living-room

couch to the local hospital ward is indeed a sacrifice, though not quite the sacrifice Jesus made in leaving a magnificent heaven for a smelly, messy, painful world. I imagine Jesus isn't too fond of hospitals, either. But whenever someone we love is there, he and I go together for a visit.

THERE IS NO FEAR IN LOVE

The Bible says that perfect love casts out fear (1 John 4:18). When we understand God's perfect love for us, we will respond to God with complete and childlike trust, no matter what the circumstances. What causes you to fret or even tremble? Open the Bible, take another look at Jesus, and discover that he is big enough to protect you no matter what challenge you are facing.

But even though I read my Bible and know God, I'm still afraid at times. I've been afraid I don't possess the capability to accomplish my God-given tasks. This fear causes me to hesitate and doubt, as so many Bible heroes such as Moses and Gideon did when God called them to a task too big for them to handle. But I've learned that all things are possible with God, so I can persevere with confidence in his abilities and his empowerment.

Fear and selfishness sometimes join together against the will of God for me. I've been afraid that if our family gives "too much," there won't be enough left for our needs. But as I've practiced giving, God has taught me that his supplies are endless and that he is faithful to provide what we need.

Fear and selfishness sometimes join together against the will of God for me.

I've been afraid of pain and of the unknown. But Jesus helps me to walk on through dark and scary places to get to my destination. Pressing on through our fear to courageous faith takes practice and patience.

One of the first verses I've taught my children is Psalm 56:3: "When I am afraid, I will trust in you." This verse has often been a resting place for me, especially during my bout with cancer.

There are few things more frightening to hear than the words "You have cancer." When I first heard them, I literally shook. Then I cried. Then I got alone with Jesus. In my imagination I stared intensely into his eyes. Then, from deep within the reality of my relationship with him, I asked out loud, "Jesus, what do you have to say about this?" His answer was distinct. It was brief. It was to the point. And it was all I needed: *Fear not.* That was enough for me. I knew it was the Lord, for with the words came the power to live with cancer and not with fear. To all who ask, he imparts a faith that acts as a bridge over which we can safely walk above the tumultuous floods of fear that seek to drown us.

Fear is the opposite of faith, and we know that without faith it is impossible to please God. Pray for more faith and love, and God's presence will cause fear to flee, even when the worst we can imagine comes upon us.

LOVE OVERCOMES THE FEAR OF REJECTION

One of the biggest roadblocks to living a life of love is the fear of rejection. What if I love someone and that person doesn't love me back? What if I am vulnerable and someone takes advantage of that or even despises my overtures of love? God faces that every day and keeps right on shining his love on the just and the unjust. His love is constant and unconditional.

One of the biggest roadblocks to living a life of love is the fear of rejection.

Sometimes I hesitate to share something I know the Lord wants me to share for fear I'll be rejected. My membership on various boards and committees sometimes places me in meetings where the others have a Ph.D. or Th.D. after their name. When a conflict arises, we practice good therapeutic principles. Once, when it was my turn to speak, I couldn't stop the tears from streaming down my face. I felt so embarrassed. None of these dignified committee members had ever cried in a meeting. I was mortified, but I persevered in speaking what seemed right. When I finished, they picked up where they had left off, going right back into therapeutic mode. I felt foolish and ineffective.

The next day someone I was sure had misunderstood me said, "What you said was strong and right, but it was your tears that made me hear it." And I had thought my tears kept people from hearing me! Love may appear foolish, but sincere love is strong and walks hand in hand with wisdom. Those who love need never be afraid they have nothing useful to offer. Any small offering given in love is enough.

Henri Nouwen writes in *Beyond the Mirror:*

> The great spiritual task facing me is to so fully trust that I belong to God that I can be free in the world—free to speak even when my words are not received; free to act even when my actions are criticized, ridiculed, or considered useless; free also to receive love from people and to be grateful for all the signs of God's presence in the world. I am convinced that I will truly be able to love the world when I fully believe that I am loved far beyond its boundaries.

A clear view of God's love keeps everything in perspective. When I'm about to speak to a crowd I find intimidating, perhaps a group of learned professors or pastors, and I feel inadequate for the task, I try to picture us all from our Father's perspective. Perhaps he sees us as little children, skipping along barefoot on the dusty road of life, dressed in tattered overalls, trying to keep up with Jesus, each one grabbing for one of his hands and showing him treasures of leaves and rocks we've found along the way. Every believer travels the same road to heaven, no matter what road we travel in life.

Fear of rejection seems the worst when it comes to our own families. It's not easy to give someone you love a Christian book and have it returned forcefully and immediately back to you or to answer a question biblically and be seen as a pompous know-it-all when you thought someone really wanted your opinion. I'm usually quiet about the differences between my beliefs and those of others, choosing instead to fight spiritual battles in the spiritual realm of prayer. But sometimes the situation demands that I speak God's truth out loud. Then I must remember that what my family thinks of me matters little in the light of eternity. What they think of Jesus will mean everything when they reach the threshold of eternity. Then every knee will bow to our Lord and Savior, both the knees that knelt daily and the knees that refused to bend. We will all appear before the judgment throne of Christ. I must remember our common destination and help to prepare those I love most by faithfully declaring and living God's Word.

I think the worst aspect of hell is that those who choose to go there first experience the judgment throne of Christ. Hell must be to feel God's splendid love emanating from the heart of Christ, to want to be warmed by that light forever, and to know that you will never again be anywhere near it. I constantly pray for wisdom and courage in representing Jesus to those closest to me.

I also want to be willing to reach out to people I don't know with the message of God's love. Many intrepid souls go "witnessing" or "canvassing" or do door-to-door evangelism. To those people I say, "God bless your precious hearts!" This is laying down your lives, not even for your friends, but for strangers.

While I was still living for this world, hurtling unknowingly toward a terrible destination, God sent an ambassador to the streets to tell absolute strangers that God was calling them home. That young man overcame the fear of rejection in order to snatch some from the impending fires of judgment. His selfless, fearless love introduced me to the love of Jesus. The course of my life and of many others changed. The population of heaven grew. For the sake of Jesus, for the sake of souls, for the sake of eternity, let's requisition more love in our fight against fear and intimidation.

Are there goals in your life, worthy goals, that you are not pursuing because of a roadblock of fear? Are there things you've wanted to say or wanted to do that bring waves of apprehension? We can't allow fear to be the deciding factor in whether or not we see our dreams come true. God is the deciding factor in every equation. Ask him to overcome your fear with the antidote of love.

This is a sane, wholesome, practical working faith: That it is a man's business to do the will of God; second, that God himself takes on the care of that man; and third, that therefore that man ought never to be afraid of anything.

GEORGE MACDONALD, *The Book of Positive Quotations*

God has not given us a spirit of fear and timidity,
but of power, love, and self-discipline.
2 TIMOTHY 1:7, NLT

Dear Lord, vanquish fear from my thoughts. Give me a heart
full of bravery, full of conviction, full of the tremendous power
of love. Let me be one who runs to the battle, certain of victory
in your name. In the powerful name of Jesus, amen.

fifteen

LOVE AND WAR

using the most effective weapon of spiritual warfare

Love brought Moses from the king of Egypt's courts to the slave quarters of the Israelites to serve and save his people. David's fervent love for God emboldened him to defend God's people from Goliath and the Philistines. It was love that compelled Jesus to leave a perfect heaven and come to suffer the cruelties of the cross. The apostles' love for souls caused them to suffer many hardships in order to traverse the known world with the story of God's love.

There have been many other tales of valiant, victorious love told by the lives of true followers of Jesus whose dedication to love has astonished their world. God's love is a force of tremendous power and might. Faith is the arrow, and love is the bow that guides it. Faith and love equip us for the battles over people's souls, battles with temptation, with discouragement, with weakness, with doubt. Faith alone cannot win the battle, for love is what puts faith into action.

FAITH WORKS THROUGH COMPASSIONATE LOVE

Since God healed me of cancer, my prayers for healing of others have greatly increased. Before becoming ill, I prayed simply out of obedience to the Word of God. But after experiencing a life-threatening illness myself, I pray with empathy and compassion. There is a difference between sympathy and compassion. Sympathy walks a mile with a friend. Compassion walks all the way to the destination.

Sympathy walks a mile with a friend. Compassion walks all the way to the destination.

Nothing engenders true compassion like empathy, feeling for someone because you have experienced the same thing. The areas where God has equipped me to serve are areas where I have been both wounded and healed. Not just wounded, but wounded and healed. It is in those places where we have experienced God's healing that our understanding, empathy, and compassion have been strengthened enough to help others. Compassion doesn't just feel *for* someone, it feels *with* them. Compassion doesn't just wonder what's wrong with someone, it wonders where that person is hurting and how we can help. Compassion intercedes as if our own lives depend on the intercession.

Obedience is noble. Faith pleases God. But add love and compassion, and your prayer will not just touch the hem of Jesus' garments. Your prayer will touch his heart.

THE WINNING WARFARE OF LOVE

Perhaps you've never thought of love and compassion as weapons in a winning arsenal against forces of evil. When we think of spiritual warfare, we usually think of armor, faith, fasting, angels, demons, battles, intercession, perseverance, warring in the heavenlies, and principalities. I haven't heard or read much about the role of love in spiritual warfare, although I have seen it defeat the schemes of the enemy where nothing else could prevail. Love seems to be a sadly neglected weapon in the arsenal of spiritual warfare. How many battles could have been won if love had led the vanguard?

Consider the battle over abortion, the most grievous of our nation's sins. It's a noble cause to stand up for the lives of those who cannot speak for themselves. But some have deafened the ears of their adversaries by their strident denunciations and demands. Worse, some who claim to be Christians have picked up the enemy's weapons and fought with hate, venom, and even murder. This wins no converts to the cause of the unborn.

Norma McCorvey, the "Roe" in the infamous 1973 *Roe v. Wade* decision that opened the floodgates of abortion in this country, was a strident proponent of abortion and often spoke for feminist and pro-abortion groups. She says that protests and demonstrations only made her position more firm. Then Operation Rescue moved into an office next to the abortion clinic where she worked. A little girl named Emily, a daughter of one of the pro-life clinic workers, befriended her. And that little girl's love won her heart. She took Norma to church. Norma then entered into dialogue and eventually a discipling relationship with Flip Benham, the director of the office. Christian love and concern won Norma's heart to the Lord and eventually to the pro-life cause. Love did what protest alone could not do. Love changed a heart, and the mind followed.

Al and Judy Howard's work at His Nesting Place in Long Beach, California, is another example of how to approach this volatile social issue with the healing balm of love. They opened their own home and later a professionally staffed facility for women who wanted to avoid an abortion but saw no other way. They and other "missionaries to the unborn" stand for untold hours in front of abortion clinics, not protesting or threatening, but offering a loving alternative. His Nesting Place even takes in whole families with several children, giving them tender love and practical help, often for the first time in their lives.

The facility has developed into a beautiful complex, with a church, a large swimming pool, a playground, a nursery, job training, courses for credit, and everything the mothers need to see them through their pregnancies and the early years of their babies' lives. Churches, both Catholic and Protestant, help the Howards in their loving endeavors. The compassionate love that burns in Al's and Judy's hearts touches and changes lives.

Compassion is love in action. The Gospel accounts tell of Jesus' compassion as he feeds the multitudes or teaches them or heals them. Notice these examples from the Gospel of Mark:

Filled with compassion, Jesus reached out his hand and touched the man. "I am willing," he said. "Be clean!" (Mark 1:41)

When Jesus landed and saw a large crowd, he had compassion on them, because they were like sheep without a shepherd. So he began teaching them many things. (Mark 6:34)

"I have compassion for these people; they have already been with me three days and have nothing to eat." (Mark 8:2)

Jesus' works of compassion attracted the crowds who came to hear the truth that set them free.

Years ago Jay and I read in *Christianity Today* about John Wessels, a young man from Otego, New York, whose ministry is to play guitar, sing songs, and pray with the comatose and their families. He began with one family he knew; then word spread, and God opened the doors of hospitals and rehabilitation centers to him.

We were so touched by this humble ministry that we contacted John and have since become friends. John and Gail Wessels' own hearts have been broken through their ordeals in the hospital with their first son, John Samuel, who loved Jesus with all his heart and died of cancer at age four.

John once spoke at Times Square Church in New York about the responsiveness of the comatose. A year later a man who had heard the speech got a call that his uncle in Puerto Rico had been injured and was in a coma. The man later called John. "Before you came to tell your stories, I would have stayed home and prayed. But I remembered what you said, got on a plane, and went to my uncle's side. I took his hand and prayed and told him the story of Jesus' love. I asked, 'If you can hear me and understand me, please squeeze my hand.' He tried to squeeze my hand, though almost imperceptibly. And two weeks later this man, who had never before trusted in God, came out of his coma. His first word was 'Hallelujah!' He had heard and received, and Jesus had begun to minister to him in his coma."

When John comes to sing love songs from God to the comatose, often the entire family, exhausted from constant care, vigilance, and grief, gathers around. John brings a touch of heaven to the worst circumstances on earth. Cancer wards filled with little children, and hospitals filled with the hopeless who have responded to nothing for months or years, are not pleasant places to visit. This kind of ministry requires a daily death to self. The love of Christ compels John and his wife, Gail, to go again and again to the most difficult of harvest fields.

After experiencing such selfless acts of compassion from the hearts of followers of Jesus, no one ever thinks of Christianity in the same way. It is no longer just another religion; it's an ongoing act of love, a way of life that gives a preview of heaven. The world needs to see more of this pure religion that reflects the heart of Jesus.

GOOD IS STRONGER THAN EVIL

The Bible is clear that the primary weapon of our warfare in the spiritual realm is our faith. But faith works through love (Galatians 5:6). Love strengthens us for the battle and keeps the goal in sight. First Thessalonians 5:8 calls faith and love a breastplate. A breastplate protects our hearts. Love lends courage for the fight; it is the compelling reason for the fight. Love for God and love for souls are the only valid reasons to engage in the intense work of spiritual warfare.

Love overcomes hate: "You have heard that the law of Moses says, 'Love your neighbor' and hate your enemy. But I say, love your enemies! Pray for those who persecute you! In that way, you will be acting as true children of your Father in heaven. For he gives his sunlight to both the evil and the good, and he sends rain on the just and on the unjust, too (Matthew 5:43-45, NLT).

Good overcomes evil: "Do not be overcome by evil, but overcome evil with good" (Romans 12:21). Love can literally disarm an evildoer. According to an Associated Press account, in September 1994 Cindy Hartman of Conway, Arkansas, walked into her house and discovered a burglar, who ripped the phone cord out of the wall and ordered her into a closet.

Hartman dropped to her knees and asked the burglar if she could pray for him. "I want you to know that God loves you and I forgive you," she said.

The burglar apologized for what he had done. Then he yelled out the door to a woman in a pickup truck, "We've got to unload all of this. This is a Christian home and a Christian family. We can't do this to them."

As Hartman remained on her knees, the burglar returned furniture he had taken from her home. Then he took the bullets out of his gun, handed the gun to Hartman, and walked out the door.

Praying for our enemies doesn't usually evoke such an immediate response. But it can change the heart of an enemy, and more important, it protects our own hearts from the toxic responses of fear, hatred, bitterness, or revenge.

How does Jesus teach us to treat our enemies? To make them prisoners of the war of love. Surround their encampments with love. Pray for them with great love. Serve them, and do good to them in love.

A LOVE FOR SOULS

Jesus' ultimate mission on earth was not to teach good things or heal the sick or model the way to live. It was to give his life as payment for our sins. It was to save souls from eternal damnation and bring them into the kingdom of God so that they might live forever with him. It is his mission and the greatest desire of his heart to bring souls into communion with himself and into life in his kingdom. The church must realign itself with our primary task—the winning of souls.

Jesus entrusted us with the great commission: "Go into all the world and preach the Good News to everyone, everywhere" (Mark 16:15, NLT). The great commandments fuel the great commission. As a new Christian, I often went street witnessing, and with good results, for God had poured out his Spirit in revival during the early seventies, the days of the Jesus movement. Young people burned with love for souls. My friends and I attended four-hour Saturday prayer meetings and prayed before and after each service with those seeking help. People found instant deliverance from drug and other addictions; runaways went home to parents; unmarried couples who were living together separated or got married; and people were set free of all manner of bondage.

The great commandments fuel the great commission.

Once, during our years of revival, I decided to take a nap instead of going street witnessing, as I had planned to do, and I dreamed that our church was traveling by bus on an evangelistic tour. Growing weary, we stopped to rest. It was a holy dream, for the young men went to sleep in one part of the building, and the young ladies were separated in another area of the building! Everyone was asleep when we were awakened by agonies of crying and moaning. We got up and went outside to discover the cause of our sleeplessness. As we approached a dark pit, the wailing and weeping increased in intensity and volume until it was nearly unbearable. I cannot describe the anguish and torment of the sound. I heard someone say, "How can we sleep until we rescue them from the pit?" Then I woke up. Almost three decades later, I still tremble at the memory of those sounds of suffering.

Christians, it's lovely to think on the glories of heaven. And it makes sense that we would think of heaven often, for we will move there one day. But there is another destination that we don't like to think about. I quickly skim over what Jesus had to say about hell. It's almost too horrific to fathom. But hell is as much a reality as heaven is. There is a heaven, and there is a hell. There is God, and there is Satan. There are ministering angels from heaven, and there are opposing angels called demons. These realities affect every man and woman whether they choose to acknowledge them or not. We must prepare others to deal with these realities. Heaven and hell are more permanent and real than the ground we walk on. We must keep eternity in our vision, or we will not be able to guide others there. Love souls enough to warn people or encourage them about the path they choose. Everyone you know here will meet up with you again at the judgment throne of Christ. Pray and say what is needed to prepare them for that day. Ask God to kindle revival in your heart until the day it breaks forth throughout the church and then the world.

THE REAL WAR

Why are we so afraid of the dark? Evil, trouble, pestilence, lawlessness, upheavals in the political and financial worlds, wars, and natural disasters will darken the last days. As the darkness deepens, the light of the believer will shine ever brighter. A candle in a room filled with light is hardly noticeable. But a candle held high on a black night can guide the way from afar. The darkness of the world in the coming days is the church's greatest opportunity. Hold on to your light, keep the oil of your lamp filled and refilled through prayer, Bible study, and fellowship with God's people, and you need never fear the dark.

Many Christians fight the increasing darkness as though it were our worst enemy. But the battles over abortion, gay rights, values, doctrinal purity, and other issues are not the real war. The real war—the war of eternal consequence—is the war for people's souls, which we must fight on the field of love, conquering one heart at a time. If God has called you to do so, stand up for God's laws in the political field, the judicial field, in denominational work, or wherever God has called you. But put love at the forefront and anger in your back pocket. It's all right to fight for righteous causes. Just don't lose sight of the precious souls of those whose opinions and lifestyles you oppose.

W. H. Griffith Thomas said, "I remember once hearing Bishop Whipple . . . utter these beautiful words: 'For thirty years I have tried to see the face of Christ in those with whom I differed.' When this spirit actuates us we shall be preserved at once from a narrow bigotry and an easy-going tolerance, from passionate vindictiveness and everything that would mar or injure our testimony for Him who came not to destroy men's lives, but to save them" (from *Streams in the Desert*).

It is possible to oppose destructive viewpoints in a spirit of love. Do you think you have the wisdom of Christ? Good! Then this is how to impart it: "The wisdom that comes from heaven is first of all pure; then peace-loving, considerate, submissive, full of mercy and good fruit, impartial and sincere" (James 3:17). Treat others with dignity and respect even if they believe and live in opposition to all you believe. Go further than that and befriend them. Some who actively protest same-sex marriage and other issues involving homosexuality have never really known and befriended a gay person. Christians must reach out to the gay community in positive ways. Support AIDS research, provide practical help after a "gay bashing" incident, correct those who make denigrating jokes about gay people. Be kind and friendly to people who happen to be gay.

The old adage "Hate the sin, and love the sinner" sounds trite and insincere to the world because so often only the first half—"hate the sin"—is ever realized. Find a sinner to love, and show by your actions that you love that person. Jesus hung out with "publicans and sinners." Let's make friends with those who need us most.

Some in the church also need understanding acceptance. They may struggle with sexual issues but won't bring their struggles to light because of the rejecting attitudes so pervasive in the church. Many who struggle with such things have felt more accepted and welcome in a gay bar than in the average church. God's love is for everyone. I know what God's Word says about the judgment to come on those who pervert God's holy laws concerning love, sex, and marriage. And I tremble for some who are very precious to me and are facing that judgment. I hope to snatch some of these from the fires of that judgment by loving them with respect, courtesy, and consideration and by praying without ceasing.

Never enter a battle with the wrong armor. In 1 Samuel 17 we read the story of David preparing for battle with Goliath. He tried on Saul's armor, but had he kept it on, he would have lost the battle. We can't fight with worldly armor. It doesn't fit; it was not made for the godly, and we can't fight using our foe's equipment. Fleshly weapons—anger, intimidation, threats, violence, retaliation, revenge—fail. We must fight spiritual battles in the spiritual realm in a spiritual way. Pick up the weapons God gave us: faith, hope, patience, endurance, gentleness, kindness, meekness, and above all, love. Love works. Love wins.

Darkness cannot drive out darkness; only light can do that.
Hate cannot drive out hate; only love can do that.
DR. MARTIN LUTHER KING JR.,
The Autobiography of Martin Luther King, Jr.

But you, O Sovereign Lord, deal well with me for your name's sake;
out of the goodness of your love, deliver me.
PSALM 109:21

Dear Lord, give me grace to love my enemies. Let me triumph
in the battle for love: first that love would conquer me,
my thoughts, my words, my plans, my deeds. Then, send me out,
armed with your love, to win the daily skirmishes and the great
battles of life. In Jesus' name, amen.

sixteen

PITFALLS ON THE PATH OF LOVE

showing true love God's way

Our intrinsically selfish nature makes it easy to veer off the path of love at times. That is just what will happen if we don't keep our eyes on the goal. The goal is not living a better life. The goal is not blessing other people. The goal is not to be a good person. The goal is not even love. The goal that will keep us on the path of love is having an authentic, vibrant relationship with God, the Father; his Son and our Lord, Jesus Christ; and our helper, the Holy Spirit.

Genuine, altruistic love grows out of our love relationship with God. Fix your eyes on Jesus, the author and finisher of our faith. Then you will avoid these common pitfalls in the pursuit of love.

PITFALL 1: WORSHIPING LOVE RATHER THAN THE LOVER OF OUR SOULS

Even the ideal of love can become an idol. Some fall into the trap of worshiping the gift rather than the giver. We can idealize and idolize love and our limited human understanding of what love is rather than God, the giver of life and love. Even love is not the greatest thing in the universe. It is God, with all his aspects, attributes, and qualities, whom we are to worship and seek after. A thorough study or even one good read-through of the Bible illustrates that God is not only a God of love but also a God of jealousy, anger, righteousness, judgment, and justice, among other attributes. God is love, but it does not follow that love is God. God is God, and only he deserves our adoration, praise, and devotion.

PITFALL 2: CREATING A LOVE THAT FITS OUR CULTURE

The most highly esteemed value of our current American culture seems to be tolerance and unthinking acceptance of just about any variation in lifestyle. The word *sin* has become an anachronism. Just watch any television talk show, and observe seemingly sane folks clapping madly for the man dressed up like Madonna who is now sleeping with his ex-wife's brother.

Christians owe their primary allegiance and conformity to a different culture—the kingdom of God. We must not presume to project this world's values onto the character and nature of God's love. God is love, and the Bible says that love is kind and patient. It does not say love is tolerant or accepting of anything and everything. Do not mistake God's kindness and patience for tolerance or, worse, for indifference. God is patient, desiring every man and woman to come to repentance. But the Bible also says, "Notice how God is both kind and severe. He is severe to those who disobeyed, but kind to you as you continue to trust in his kindness" (Romans 11:22, NLT). Judgment comes in its time.

God's love does not always fill us with good feelings. Love is sometimes painful for the recipient. When my young son has a splinter embedded in his hand, I don't just kiss the boo-boo and whisper soft reassurances. I grab the tweezers, tell him to look away, and do what I need to do to get the offending splinter out of his hand. Then, while he is still howling, I apply a disinfectant, which stings. After the pain his loving mother has just inflicted on him, he gets the Disney Band-Aids and the kisses and the glass of chocolate milk. But at first it hurts, it may involve blood, my son may temporarily hate me—and it's still love.

God's love doesn't often resemble anything conjured up for Valentine's Day. It doesn't always come wrapped in soft pink; sometimes it seems to come in angry red or ominous black. It's not always sweet. It can taste harsh and even bitter. But when love is tough, it is just as valid and effective as when it is tender.

Sometimes we love like a mother bear protecting her cubs. That's fierce love. I have written letters quite unlike the letters reprinted elsewhere in this book, letters of scathing rebuke, when I felt someone was committing a terrible wrong. I have fiercely defended my friends' reputations or my children's rights. These, too, have been love letters but of a different sort. God's loving correction or redirection can also seem like anything but love.

God's love is not always sweet. It can taste harsh and even bitter. But when love is tough, it is just as valid and effective as when it is tender.

This book has sent only snapshots of what love looks like from where I live. I urge you to become faithful readers of the Bible, the authoritative book on love. When you read the Bible with a prayerful heart, you will begin to grasp the full spectrum of God's love.

PITFALL 3: GIVING LOVE TO RECEIVE LOVE

Jenny wrote sweet, encouraging notes to women at church. She gave elaborate gifts to the pastoral staff at Christmas. She worked faithfully in the nursery. People often saw her hard at work on special church projects. Then one Sunday she was gone from the church, and no one ever saw her there again. Unknown to her friends at church, a gnawing resentment had grown inside her. She had not received public recognition for her contributions. She had never received the kinds of notes she had written to others. When she had needs, no one seemed to notice them. Jenny's investment had not "paid off." She had given so much love, time, and attention, but it did not result in the recognition, affection, and gratitude she craved. Her need for love eventually choked her desire to give it.

Wrong motivations can thwart our desire to live a genuinely loving life. It is easy to fall into the trap of giving love in order to receive love. The desire to be loved is one of the strongest motivators there is. I would rather be without food and water than without love. We can be thankful because those who know and walk with God need never feel unloved. We arc the apple of his eye. He loves us unconditionally. And when he looks at us, he sees wonderful, unique individuals whose every sin is hidden from his sight by a banner of love that he himself bestowed on us. Rest peacefully in the wonder of his love.

Like Jenny, we sometimes try to earn love from parents, spouses, and other relatives and friends by being loving. And while it's true that doing loving acts can be a valid way to create loving feelings, that can't be our motivation or even our expectation, for relationships do not always work out that way. Those we love the most will sometimes hurt us the most, although often unintentionally. And some will never love us or even regard us kindly, no matter how much love we lavish on them.

Learn the pure pleasure of giving love simply to express your feelings. Genuine selfless love toward children comes naturally for most parents, grandparents, aunts, and uncles. Maternal and paternal feelings of protectiveness, affection, and near adoration seem to come more easily because we aren't expecting much in return from the undeveloped personalities of the very young.

But it can be much more difficult to continually act lovingly toward a parent or sibling or other relative who is stingy with love toward you. An unloved child lives with a perpetual sadness. An unloved spouse walks through marriage fighting waves of grief. If this is your situation, my advice is to pray and endure. Pray for healing in the unloving one, in your own heart, and in the relationship, and for grace to endure until that healing comes. With God, our ability to love is not dependent on the other person's ability to love us.

Most of us don't feel completely unloved, but we may wish our parents or a spouse, a sibling, or friends loved us more. Forgive the lack, and enjoy what love you have received. If you are a parent, try to make things different for your children. Work at making the world a more lovely and loving place because you were here. Love with a pure heart, for the joy of loving, and expect nothing in return.

PITFALL 4: LOVING OUT OF SPIRITUAL PRIDE

Gwen made a loving decision to quit her job and home-school her three young children. She enjoyed the renewed closeness they were experiencing and found a sense of satisfaction and accomplishment in working together. Gwen felt she had really made the right move. She was so sure of it that she wondered about others who had made different schooling choices for their children. It bothered her that her friends weren't willing to make the sacrifices she had made. The initial satisfaction and renewed love she had found in teaching her children at home faded with each comparison she made. To make a sacrifice in love is a noble thing. To resent those who don't make the same choices we do diminishes our sacrifice and causes love to dissolve into self-righteousness.

Pride is the mortal enemy of love. True love wears a veil of humility. It walks quietly, seeking no recognition or status. It bestows gifts in secret. It seeks out the unlovely to love, the poor to show generosity, the friendless to befriend. "Love is not . . . boastful or proud" (I Corinthians 13:4, NLT).

We are not such wonderful, loving human beings that we do acts of righteousness out of the goodness of our own hearts. James 1:17 says that every good and perfect gift comes from our heavenly Father. This includes the gift of love. He imparted the great gift of love to our hard, cold hearts, so how can we take the credit for any goodness that we now impart to others?

Pride can make us feel angry with those who do not seem to love as much as we do or do not perform the works of service that we do. And lecturing those people usually doesn't motivate; it alienates. Instead, inspire others by your example rather than by exhortation or rebuke. Did the five wise virgins described in Matthew 25 spend any time berating their lazy sisters? No, their hearts were set on preparing for the bridegroom's coming. Forgive others' shortcomings, and concentrate on doing what you know is right:

> Since God chose you to be the holy people whom he loves, you must clothe yourselves with tenderhearted mercy, kindness, humility, gentleness, and patience. You must

make allowance for each other's faults and forgive the person who offends you. Remember, the Lord forgave you, so you must forgive others. And the most important piece of clothing you must wear is love. Love is what binds us all together in perfect harmony. (Colossians 3:12-14, NLT)

At our very best we are only "unworthy servants" (Luke 17:10). Love to the best of your ability, and thank God for lending you that love.

PITFALL 5: LOVING WITH A CHECKLIST MENTALITY

I used to think that parenting was a two-decade career. I do my job and then release my children into the world, finished. As any parent of grown children knows, this is ridiculous. A parent loves, worries, prays, and assists a child for life. Some children need more help than others, but none are ever "finished."

To love another is a never-ending endeavor. We can never "do enough" for those we love. At times we may experience "caregiver's burnout" and reason, *OK, I've done enough for this person now. I've extended myself beyond normal human cords of kindness.* Then another chance to show love in practical ways presents itself. Pray about it, and ask God for the necessary resources of time, energy, and compassion. Bravely say yes once again.

Love does say no at times. Love respects boundaries. It's true that love tries to say yes more often than no. But sometimes saying yes to someone's request means that we would be helping another to sin (like giving cash to a homeless alcoholic, for instance). Even then the answer doesn't have to be no. Can we find a loving alternative? How about carrying McDonald's gift certificates? Or taking the man out for lunch yourself? So often our own limited imaginations hinder us, and we think that every dilemma has only one or two solutions. But God is endlessly creative—just think of the aardvark or the rhinoceros!—and he can give us creative solutions to every situation. Ask and you shall receive.

Even after death, love is not finished. Don't you still love and long for your loved ones who are no longer here? Our opportunities to express love to them may be gone, but the loving feelings remain. It's good to think about those who have gone before us, especially when we know that we loved them well and that they felt our love. But sometimes thoughts of those who are gone bring painful but necessary lessons.

I had a friend who died of breast cancer. While she was ill, I kept thinking of what I could do to cheer her, but I allowed my own interests to hinder me from fulfilling my good intentions. She died without having received much encouragement from me. The regret over my failure to translate good intentions into loving words and deeds prompted me to resolve to love more diligently. Since then, when a friend is gravely ill, I do my best to offer support and practical help.

Sometimes there is even a way to express love and honor after someone has died. When David's faithful friend Jonathan was still alive, David had promised him that he would show kindness to the members of Saul's family for Jonathan's sake. After Jonathan's death, David searched for Saul's descendants and found Mephibosheth, one of Jonathan's sons, and honored and blessed him with loving-kindness (2 Samuel 9). Even after others are gone, we can show love by supporting causes our friends believed in, carrying on a work they loved, or imitating the best characteristics of their lives and giving them credit as our example. Love endures, even beyond the grave.

PITFALL 6: FEELING THAT THOSE WE LOVE "OWE" US

How many times have we been caught up in anger and resentment over the unrequited loves of everyday life? Do any of these comments sound familiar?

"Hey, I backed off to let that car in, and the driver didn't even wave to thank me!"

"I baby-sat her children dozens of times for free, and now that I have children, she doesn't return the favor even once."

"I gave up my entire career to raise my daughter, and now she's not speaking to me because I can't drive her to the mall."

"I give that guy a ride to work every day; then he bad-mouths me to the boss. He can take the bus from now on."

Unless we do an act of love completely without obligation, it is not an act of love but an act of commerce. Our sacrifice becomes merely payment in advance for some sort of reciprocation.

In earlier years I was disheartened to see how quickly others forget our acts of love and sacrifice on their behalf. When our church suffered a split, people I dearly loved left our church, apparently without any balanced examination of the facts. Whole families listened to slander and left without ever asking the pastor if the accusations were true. My husband and I had tried always to be there for our church members, coming to their sides at the hospital or the morgue, caring for their children, listening and praying into the night, and offering practical help when babies were born or people were ill. But in the excitement of conflict, slander, and gossip, the evidence of our love for them was forgotten. When I lapsed into self-pity, I painfully discovered what my true motivation for service had been. I had given much, expecting love and loyalty in return. I had failed to love unconditionally, extravagantly, with enough love to bless people even in my disappointment with them. I had to do some serious examination of my motivations for ministry. When we invest in others in hopes of getting a return on this earth, we may lose our investment. But when we invest those same acts of service in the kingdom, for Jesus' sake, we will never lose our reward.

Jesus warned that in the last days, "because of the increase of wickedness, the love of most will grow cold" (Matthew 24:12). When others are hateful and ungrateful, it is a great temptation to stop loving in order to protect ourselves from pain and disappointment later. The avoidance of pain is a popular but vain pursuit. And avoiding love to avoid pain also causes us to miss out on the wonders of love. Godly love willingly endures pain for the honor of suffering with Christ and understanding just a bit of the rejection he suffered. I am learning to "serve wholeheartedly, as if you were serving the Lord, not men" (Ephesians 6:7) and to "do everything in love" (1 Corinthians 16:14).

Now when people I've loved leave our fellowship, I grieve for the loss of the friendship but not for any loss of investment. Nothing we do for Jesus is ever wasted. Nothing we sow into

others' lives is ever a poor investment, either. If we give extravagantly, people leave us richer and will have more to share, maybe
not with us but perhaps with others. Ephesians 6:8 says, "Remember that the Lord will reward each one of us for the good we do"
(NLT). That surely will be enough reward.

Walk hand in hand with wisdom and humility, look to Jesus
as your guide, and you will not lose your way on the path of love.

> The last temptation is the greatest treason:
> To do the right deed for the wrong reason.
> T. S. Eliot, *Murder in the Cathedral*

This is my prayer: that your love may abound more and more
in knowledge and depth of insight.
PHILIPPIANS 1:9

Dear Lord, I aspire to genuine, selfless love. This world can
distort love into a myriad of shapes and sizes that don't look
anything like love did when it came from heaven. Keep my love
true to the shape of the cross. In the name of the Savior, amen.

seventeen

A LEGACY OF LOVE

investing for eternity

Can farmers from Kansas grow a church in California? Lyle and Doris Steenis did. Back in 1948 they plotted the field, broke up the ground, sowed, watered, and finally reaped. Folks back home told the tale of how Lyle saw a cloud formation spelling "P C" in a clear Kansas sky. They thought the sign in the sky meant "Plow corn." Lyle said it meant "Preach Christ." So he diligently followed what he discerned as the Lord's direction. He moved to Redondo Beach when it was nothing but sand dunes and fields and built a little church with his own hands. Lyle and Doris made their home in the church nursery while they prayed for souls and for revival and struggled to grow a congregation.

By 1969 Brother Steenis was pastor to about three hundred middle-class, middle-aged family folks. He fasted and prayed for revival and tried to bring it about twice a year with visiting evangelists. There was spiritual growth and numerical growth. God was at work in their lives.

But, as God likes to do, he had saved the best for last. And as he also likes to do, he sent an answer to prayer in disguise. In the midst of their nice family congregation, something messy happened. It was chaotic. It was unorthodox. It was almost unrecognizable. It was revival.

Some kids from the love generation found Brother Steenis and Jesus, in that order, and knew they had found real love. They brought their friends, and soon the services were overflowing with barefoot, long-haired types wearing love beads and placing their drugs and rock-and-roll albums on the altar for Jesus. They came half-dressed, and some of the newer ones still smoked cigarettes out in the parking lot. Then they wanted to pray till all hours of the night, and they moved in together for fellowship till their homes were so full that it looked as if communes were cropping up. Just what was this, anyway, a hippie church? a cult? a commune? Soon most of the tithe-paying families were on their way, delivering warnings of doom at the back door as they left.

WHEN ALL HEAVEN BROKE LOOSE

Brother Steenis was still an old Kansas farmer at heart and didn't know much about cultural relevance or the unique characteristics of this generation. But he knew how to hang on to God when all heaven broke loose. He didn't try to understand it or control it. He went on preaching the Word of God faithfully. Before services he could be found in the prayer room on his knees, holding hands with Doris. The young people didn't know he was holding on for dear life.

He knew what was happening was of God, but why did God have to be so strange? Why wasn't everything being done decently and in order as before? Now *that* looked like church. What he had now was sending the denominational authorities— along with the media—over for a skeptical look-see.

Brother Steenis's little church ended up hosting fifty to one hundred "seekers" every service. They held church services almost every day of the week. *Look, Life,* and *Time* magazines all featured this little church with the non-seeker-friendly name, Bethel Tabernacle, in their articles about the Jesus movement. I remember it all, for Lyle Steenis was the man who took my hand in his and led me in prayer, ushering me out of darkness and into the light.

Lyle and Doris had prayed for revival. They were looking forward to seeing the church grow and to the denomination inviting Lyle to be the featured speaker at the next holy convocation. Instead, church became a sort of heavenly train station where literally thousands got on board, met Christ, and then moved on. Established Christians came not to help but to "discern the spirits." But no matter. Over the clamor of confusion, Lyle could hear the angels rejoicing, not in solos, not in quartets, but in choirs.

Brother Steenis used to say, "My only compensation for a life in the ministry is souls." He was well compensated. He watched over his untidy, immature flock for three more years until one day the small plane he was flying went down in an accident— and he went up. After that, the fledgling believers had to grow up fast. Many went on to become mature, fruitful Christians, some as Christian workers and ministers, as I did and the man I later married. Still, even after three decades of ministry, all I know about revival is that it seldom looks neat and tidy. And the only compensation for the hard life of ministry is souls.

Lyle and Doris Steenis never had any children of their own to receive their legacy. But their legacy of love, passion for prayer, hard work and determination, and burning love for souls lives on as seed scattered all over the earth, as love planted in the hearts of thousands who love the Lord and love others to this day. Everyone leaves a legacy. The wise leave a legacy of love.

YOUR LAST GIFT

A legacy is a gift to the future. Some leave a legacy through their achievement. For instance, Maria Woodworth-Etter accomplished the formidable task of ministering as a traveling evangelist beginning in the late 1800s, a time when women in ministry were rarely accepted. Others leave a legacy through the work they establish. Clara Barton's legacy lives on through the organization she founded in 1821, the American Red Cross. Some leave a legacy of ideas, original thought, or old thoughts phrased in new ways that change the way others think and act. Keith and Melody Green and their work, Last Days Ministries, helped the young Jesus movement grow up. Through their music and impassioned writing and speaking, they redefined the call to missions in language their generation could understand.

Some famous folks leave legacies that appear to be spectacular from the world's vantage point but make no impact whatsoever on the kingdom of God. What surprises the Judgment Day will hold. Many who are unknowns here are well known in heaven. There we will be admiring legacies of giving, of loving, of serving, of patient perseverance in the face of adversity, of sacrifice, of humility, of obedience. The most important question, after the question of whether or not we are washed in the blood of Jesus, will be, "Did you do what I asked you to do?" If the Lord asked you to remain single, teach school for forty years, and spend your retirement caring for your aging parent's needs and you did it with love, your reward may be as great as that of someone as prominent as Billy Graham. Our lives of service are just as important if they are done in obedience, with loving faithfulness.

WE'RE ALL HISTORY MAKERS

Men and women whose names we recognize have changed the face of history. But we need to realize that we *all* change the face of history with each life we affect. There is no small legacy of love. Every life lived in love is a triumphant accomplishment in the kingdom of God.

We all change the face of history with each life we affect.

If you think you're being watched or followed, you may not be paranoid. People are watching you. People are following you. I was surprised last Christmas to learn how attentive my children really are. We were shopping when we saw someone selling sprigs of mistletoe. Alex reminded me, "Remember last year when you asked that little boy why he was selling mistletoe and he said he was raising money to buy a present for his mom? Remember when you gave him a twenty-dollar bill and said he was a good boy and he cried and smiled at the same time? That still makes me happy." I had forgotten all about that, but Alex remembered.

My daughter Amanda is helping to support herself through college right now by working as a waitress. She works for believers, so she is able to write "Jesus cares about you!" on every check. She learned this as she watched her parents write that same phrase as we sign each credit card receipt and add a generous tip to underline the thought. I am constantly amazed at how my growing children have incorporated what their parents do into their lives. People are observing our lives, especially young people. When they look back, will their memories be life-lifting memories of love? It's up to us.

My growing children have never said, "I remember that lecture you gave." They have said, "I remember when you did . . ." Love teaches not by lecture but by example. Love looks better on a model than on a page. We learn love primarily through our emotions, not through our reasoning.

Hebrews 10:24 is a life-guiding verse for me: "Let us consider how we may spur one another on toward love and good deeds."

Think about the lives of great lovers you have known. They do spur us on toward love and good deeds. The ones who inspire me also warm me against the chill of the world. They free me when I feel stingy. They hold my hand on the uphill path of love. They inspire me when I'm weary. Their legacy of love lives in my heart.

TAKE STOCK OF YOUR LEGACY

To focus our lives, all we have to do is imagine our funerals or memorial services. "Death is the destiny of every man," said the writer of Ecclesiastes. "The living should take this to heart" (Ecclesiastes 7:2). Have you ever imagined what your own funeral will be like? Who will be there, and what will people share about your life? It is moral bankruptcy to gain wealth but never be known for philanthropy. It is emptiness to excel at your chosen career but leave your family feeling abandoned. It is cruel to show your friends a good time and never show them the way to eternal life. Will your friends talk about your wild times together and all the fun you had, or will they weep in gratitude for the way you pointed them to Jesus? Will they talk about what a self-made man you were, what an entrepreneur? Or will people extol your generosity and how you couldn't give enough away to help others? What one attribute will characterize the way your life is summed up?

Where will your treasure be stored up? Here, hoarded up to protect you in this life that is so quickly finished? Or in heaven, given away to good works and godly people who will use it for God's kingdom? What legacy will you leave to those who remain? Can others look to your life for lessons in love that teach them how to live in harmony with God and how to die with sweet peace?

Every day you can create your legacy of love by living a lifestyle of love. Give away all the love you have to give, entrusting it to the hearts of those you love. From the seed of a sacrifice of love, a great harvest of love will grow.

Dr. Charles Shepson, founder of Fairhaven Ministries, a clergy care retreat in Tennessee, tells the story of an aspiring missionary who studied for many years to work in India. She loved the country, loved the people, and longed to serve them with her whole life. Within a short time of her arrival in India a telegram arrived. Her sister and brother-in-law had been killed in an accident. Would she come home to care for the orphaned children? She relinquished her heart's desire, and instead of sacrificing for India's multitudes, she sacrificed her lifelong goal and became the mother of three grieving children.

She tenderly loved them. They grew to love her. They grew to love her God. They grew to love her beloved India. Today all three are grown and serve with their families as missionaries in India. That is what happens to our love when we surrender it to God. He multiplies it over and over until the coming of the Lord closes the accounts.

SETTING ASIDE A LEGACY FOR ETERNITY

There is an earthly legacy of love that lives on through our giving, our children, our works, and the lives we touch. There is also an eternal legacy that we store up for God's glory in heaven. I often say to my grown daughters, "Be careful how you treat your forty-year-old self. You are creating her right now, at eighteen and twenty. Keep reading and learning. Wear your sunscreen. Take your vitamins. Treat your body with respect. I know you don't believe that you'll be forty someday, but you will. Take good care

of your forty-year-old self. Love her now, and she will be a blessing to you."

How much more do we need to be careful how we treat
our souls, our eternal selves. We'll be living with the consequences
of our current actions and attitudes for an eternity. We don't want
to be ashamed at the judgment seat of Christ because God gave us
ten talents and we only used eight, or because it took so long to
forgive others, or because of all the chances to love that we over-
looked or purposely passed by.

We are all allotted the same amount of time to live. We
were created for eternity, no matter what age we achieve here.
Every soul, born and unborn, that had life, is destined to live in
eternity, and God has issued an invitation to spend it with him.

MORE LOVE, BECAUSE YOU LIVED

I used to think I wanted people to say on the day I die, "Today
there is less love in the world." Now I know that this is exactly the
opposite of what I desire to achieve. I want there to be more love
in the world—more love in the lives I touched and the lives of all
they touch, more love because of the way I lived. I want a harvest of
love to keep growing from the small seeds I sowed. My life will have
been worthwhile if I succeeded in encouraging others toward more
love and good deeds.

Let's continually requisition heaven for vast supplies of
charity, compassion, benevolence, affection, and loving-kindness
and pass it out to a world in short supply of such valuable riches.
Show the way to the source of love. Encourage others toward deeds
of kindness. Love others deeply, with a pure heart. Win souls who
will love the Lord.

Redeemed souls, good deeds, warm memories, a fruitful
life worthy of imitation, love that lives on in the hearts of others,
eternal riches in glory, this is the honorable legacy of a lifestyle
of love. A love-filled life means a lasting legacy here and in
eternity. God is going to comfort us after our labors. He will
say, "Well done, good and faithful servant. Enter into the joy
of your Lord."

Significance is seldom achieved when aimed at directly.
It is a serendipity of a life well-lived.

JERRY COOK, FROM *The Connection*, A NEWSLETTER OF CHRISTIAN
COUNSELING MINISTRIES, BUENA VISTA, COLORADO (FALL 1999)

*Those who are wise will shine like the brightness of the heavens, and those who lead
many to righteousness, like the stars for ever and ever.*
DANIEL 12:3

*Dear Lord, make me wise in the matters of eternity.
Let me understand what the will of the Lord is, and make me
faithful to accomplish your will. Make me to abound in love,
to excel at love, to be victorious in love, to leave a legacy of love.
Help me to earn a magnificent, jewel-studded crown so that
I will have something worthy of you to cast at your feet.
In the name of King Jesus, amen.*

LOVE THROUGH ME

Love through me, Love of God,
There is no love in me;
O Fire of love, light Thou the love
That burns perpetually.

Flow through me, Peace of God,
Calm river flow until
No wind can blow, no current stir
A ripple of self-will.

Shine through me, Joy of God,
Make me like Thy clear air
That Thou dost pour Thy colours through,
As though it were not there.

O blessed Love of God,
That all may taste and see
How good Thou art, once more I pray
Love through me, even me.

AMY CARMICHAEL

NOTE TO THE READER

I would love for you to share your own stories, ideas, and positive experiences. Write and share them with me.

Linda Riley
Living Word Fellowship
2424 Moreton Street
Torrance, CA 90505-5311

Love,
Linda

ABOUT THE AUTHOR

Linda Riley is the founder of Called Together Ministries, an organization serving ministry families. Linda authored a column, "For Heaven's Sake," for *Leadership Journal* for several years and is currently a freelance writer on family and ministry issues. She also serves on the board of Ministry Wives Network International. Linda and her husband, Jay, a pastor, are foster parents and adoptive parents and keep very busy raising eight children. They live in Torrance, California.

Love is being primarily concerned with the well-being of another. Linda has given us invaluable advice and biblical incentives to let God love our world through us.

—JILL BRISCOE, SPEAKER AND AUTHOR OF *Prayer That Works*

It's easy to talk about love—easier than loving. Linda has done a great job in helping us put our lives where our mouths are. She helps all of us give to others what God has given to us—love. The world (and especially the Christian world) would change if we would all read and live by this book.

—STEPHEN ARTERBURN, FOUNDER OF NEW LIFE CLINICS AND WOMEN OF FAITH

Linda's book, *The Call to Love,* challenges me on a deep level, and I highly recommend it to anyone. Linda's words encourage me, confront my own heart and motives, and remind me that there is no greater quest in life than to pursue this greatest of all callings—to love.

—NANCIE CARMICHAEL, FORMER EDITOR OF *Virtue* MAGAZINE AND AUTHOR OF *The Deeper Life*

I found myself smiling yet deeply moved as I read *The Call to Love.* It's a winsome, convicting read. Linda Riley's wit and practical advice pull the reader in through colorful stories out of her life and the lives of others. Loving isn't academic for Linda. Having known her for many years, I admire her daily choice to love in sacrificial ways.

—GAIL MACDONALD, AUTHOR OF *In His Everlasting Arms*

My wife, Heather, and I welcome the opportunity to commend warmly to readers everywhere Linda Riley's new book, *The Call to Love: Living the Great Commandments.* The apostle Paul sums up Christian doctrine and duty in those famous words "Now abide faith, hope, love, these three; but the greatest of these is love"; and then he adds, "Pursue love" (1 Corinthians 13:13–14:1). We are to follow after love as our "calling." This is why Jesus said, "By this all will know that you are My disciples, if you have love for one another" (John 13:35). Linda has spelled this out in a biblical, practical, and readable book that should challenge the heart of everyone. There is no greater message for our times or troubles than the call to love. Our prayer is that God will use the book to the blessing of thousands who live and die in a loveless world.

—DR. STEPHEN OLFORD, FOUNDER OF THE STEPHEN OLFORD CENTER
FOR BIBLICAL PREACHING AND AUTHOR OF *Time for Truth*